FISHING
for beginners

by Allen Edwards
and Michael Prichard

COLLINS
GLASGOW·LONDON

Introduction

This book tells the young fisherman — or a beginner of any age — all he needs to know when he first takes up angling for coarse fish or fishing from the sea shore.

Long, long ago fishing was a simple matter of a stick, a string and a bait on a hook. Today things are very different. The beginner is faced with a bewildering assortment of tackle and gear and unless he takes expert advice he can spend a lot of money, waste a lot of time — and not catch a single fish.

In these pages Mike Prichard and Allen Edwards — both top fishermen with European reputations — explain the basics in simple terms. Fishing, of course, is not a simple sport. The good fisherman has to know quite a lot about the habits of fish and a great deal about the water and feeding environments in which the various species of fish thrive.

Fishing is an international sport and more and more people are taking their rods and tackle with them on their holidays.

People from the Continental countries fish in Britain and the British are discovering the delights of fishing for different species such as the nase and the orfe in French and North European freshwaters and the saupe and common Mediterranean sea bream further down the coastline in the summer waters of the south. This is, in fact, a Common Market beginner's guide to angling.

There are dozens of drawings to make the technicalities you must master as simple as possible — and superbly accurate fish illustrations by Dr Dietrich Burkel, an icthyologist (and that means an expert on fish) of international standing, and by Keith Linsell, who did all the illustrations of tackle and techniques.

Here, then, is the perfect handbook for beginners — and even the expert might pick up the odd tip or two.

Read it carefully, follow its advice and, above all, have fun! Fishing is a great sport. But to get the best from it we must approach it with respect — and understand the marvellous world of fish and water and play our part in keeping the environment clean and sweet and healthy.

Tight lines!

© 1978 William Collins Sons and Company Limited
All rights reserved
First published in 1978
Fifth impression 1980
Published by William Collins Sons and Company Limited
Glasgow and London
Printed in Great Britain
ISBN 0 00 106246 8

Created and designed by Berkeley Publishers Limited, 9 Warwick Court, London WC1R 5DJ

Contents

From stream to estuary   6
Running water   8
Fish of the rivers   10
River fish, big and small   12
Fishing tackle   14
The roach   16
Chub and dace   18
Barbel, bleak and gudgeon   20
Fishing the small streams   22
Legering in the stream   24
Canals: fisheries of the future?   26
Fishing the canals   28
Stillwaters: lake, pond and pool   30
The life cycle in stillwaters   32
The fish of stillwaters   34
Stillwater populations   36
Tackle for stillwater fishing   38
Tench fishing methods   40
Legering for tench   42
Float fishing for bream   44
Legering for big bream   46
Float fishing for rudd   48
Baits for fish   50
Fishing for carp   52
Crucian carp, roach and perch   54
Spinning for perch and pike   56
Pike fishing   58
Saltwater fishing   60
The four shorefishing habitats   62
Fishing from the shingle beach   64
The shore angler's basic tackle   66
Casting from the shore   68
Cod and whiting from beaches   70
Fishing the sandy beaches   72
Tackle for sandy beach species   74
Fishing from the rocky shore   76
Fish of the rocky shore   78
Spinning from the rocks   80
The complete shorefisher   82
Fishing from piers and harbours   84
Angling in the estuaries   86
Other species, big and small   88
Colourful visitors   90
Index   92

From stream to estuary

Water is life. All animals, including human beings, need an abundant supply of water both to drink and to keep themselves clean. Fish, of course, live out their entire lives in water. So the condition of the water they must live in is of immense importance to them.

Water reaches our rivers, streams and lakes in many ways. Much of it comes in the form of snow during the winter. Heavy rain storms put rivers into what we call "spate" – a great rush of water which tears away the bankside vegetation and earth. This upsets the regular lives of all the creatures living in the river or stream or along the banks.

Light and frequent showers that soak into the earth and seep gently into the rivers and streams provide the best sort of water supply. The steady flow of water gently flushes away the debris that gathers in rivers and streams and also washes away the polluting materials man all too often dumps in them.

The speed of a river's flow decides what sort of fish can live in the water. Game fish, such as salmon and trout, prefer the fast water that tumbles down from the high ground through mountains and moorland. This is the cleanest sort of water; it also contains more oxygen than slow-moving rivers. Trout and salmon prefer colder water than their coarse fish cousins.

A river along its course is joined by many sidestreams. This makes the river deeper and wider and slows down its rate of flow. When a river has reached this stage then roach, dace, chub and barbel will live and breed in it.

Once a river has reached the flat lands it begins to twist and wind its way. This is the sort of water in which we will find bream, tench and river carp.

When the river reaches the sea we find a mixture of fresh water and salt water. This part of a river is called an estuary. In estuaries we often find roach, a few bream, eels and trout feeding next to shoals of mullet, with flounders and the occasional bass.

In many parts of Western Europe man has created another form of waterway – the canal. Canals can be excellent fisheries for fish species that like slow-running water. Unfortunately, many canals have fallen into disuse. They silt up because no boats pass through the locks.

As the number of fishermen grows, the need for us all to maintain our rivers and canals in good condition becomes vital. It is the duty of all anglers to keep rivers and waterways fit for fish to live in and for people to live beside.

Left: The small stream, in lowland areas has a lush growth of weed and good food potential. Water levels are rarely constant so fish do not grow to large sizes.

Species in Grayling Zone: trout, grayling, salmon parr, stone loach, and Miller's Thumb.

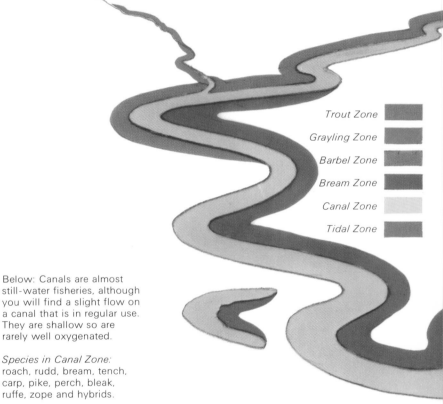

Trout Zone
Grayling Zone
Barbel Zone
Bream Zone
Canal Zone
Tidal Zone

Below: Canals are almost still-water fisheries, although you will find a slight flow on a canal that is in regular use. They are shallow so are rarely well oxygenated.

Species in Canal Zone: roach, rudd, bream, tench, carp, pike, perch, bleak, ruffe, zope and hybrids.

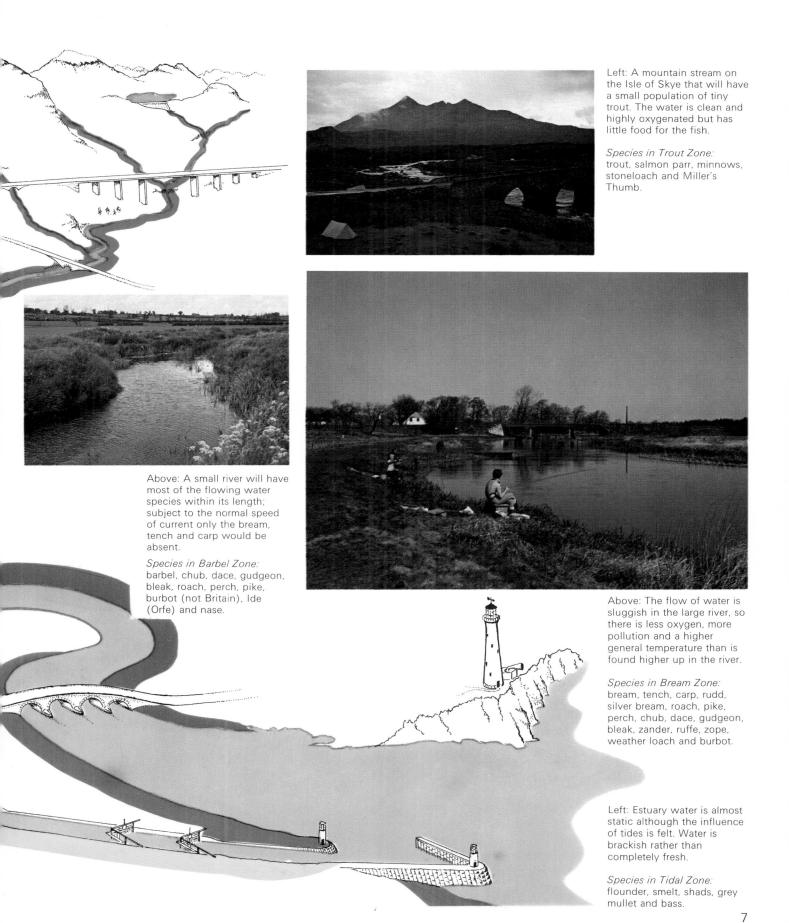

Left: A mountain stream on the Isle of Skye that will have a small population of tiny trout. The water is clean and highly oxygenated but has little food for the fish.

Species in Trout Zone: trout, salmon parr, minnows, stoneloach and Miller's Thumb.

Above: A small river will have most of the flowing water species within its length; subject to the normal speed of current only the bream, tench and carp would be absent.

Species in Barbel Zone: barbel, chub, dace, gudgeon, bleak, roach, perch, pike, burbot (not Britain), Ide (Orfe) and nase.

Above: The flow of water is sluggish in the large river, so there is less oxygen, more pollution and a higher general temperature than is found higher up in the river.

Species in Bream Zone: bream, tench, carp, rudd, silver bream, roach, pike, perch, chub, dace, gudgeon, bleak, zander, ruffe, zope, weather loach and burbot.

Left: Estuary water is almost static although the influence of tides is felt. Water is brackish rather than completely fresh.

Species in Tidal Zone: flounder, smelt, shads, grey mullet and bass.

Running water

All creatures need oxygen to breathe. Land animals and birds get oxygen from the air, drawing the air through their nostrils down into their lungs. The cleansing oxygen feeds into the bloodstream and is returned into the air as carbon dioxide. Fish also need oxygen, which is a basic element in water. Fish do not have lungs, although most fish possess a swim bladder that contains air to regulate their balance and to enable them to swim at a given depth. A fish gets oxygen by sucking in water through its mouth. This water is then passed out through openings at each side of the head. These openings, called gill-slits, have a number of fine filaments within them. These filaments take oxygen from the water as it passes out through the protective gill-cases.

Although oxygen is always present in water, sometimes the amount is reduced. Hot weather, coupled with low water levels, tend to put fish off their food. They cease to chase natural food and lie quietly, using no energy, since in this way they require less oxygen. This lethargy is common among human beings who also react like this in hot, sultry weather. Water is oxygenated in a number of ways. It absorbs oxygen from the atmosphere but oxygen is also taken in as water rushes down steep gradients or spills over waterfalls and weirs. Rain brings oxygen into the river and so do the waves whipped up by strong winds.

Fish of the salmon family need to live in water with a high oxygen content, so we find them in rivers that flow swiftly and are cold and pure. Coarse fish are to be found in slow-running waters since these fish can tolerate lower levels of oxygen. The carp and tench are two species that can exist in water with a low oxygen content.

Many forms of plant life also contribute to the oxygen supply available in water. This is brought about by a process known as photosynthesis, in which plants take in carbon dioxide during the daylight hours and expel oxygen as a life-giving product. This process is reversed at night and so creates a night-time shortage of life-giving oxygen. Unfortunately, during the late autumn, dying vegetation drops into the river, sinks to the river bed and begins to rot. The gas this produces greatly reduces the oxygen available to waterborne creatures but the first heavy rains will clear this debris away as the heavy water speeds to the sea.

River fish live on a varied supply of natural food. They will eat practically anything that is swept down the current to them. There are three basic forms of natural food. Larger fish eat smaller fish. They also eat animals that live in the river and a multitude of creatures that live on the surrounding land but which fall into the water. Then there is a wide variety of vegetable material – fine weed, the shoots of water plants and the seeds and fruits of riverside trees.

Not all fish eat the same natural foods nor do they feed in the same river bottom areas or at the same water height. The barbel grubs for its food on the river bed, rooting among the stones for grubs and worms. The trout takes insect-life both in the grub stage or as fully-winged flies. The pike, the supreme predator, eats other fish. He ambushes them from holes in the banks of the river or from thick weed beds. But the pike, along with the perch, performs a useful role as a scavenger, cleaning up all the sickly and dying fish. The predatory species of fish also stabilize the numbers of fish that are able to live in any stretch of water.

Above: Not a natural grub found at the riverside, the angler's maggot does simulate bankside larvae.

Below: Water plants are limited in distribution by the depth of water. The best example is probably the water lily.

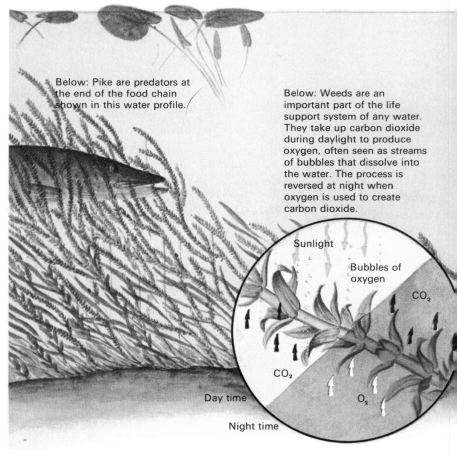

Below: Pike are predators at the end of the food chain shown in this water profile.

Below: Weeds are an important part of the life support system of any water. They take up carbon dioxide during daylight to produce oxygen, often seen as streams of bubbles that dissolve into the water. The process is reversed at night when oxygen is used to create carbon dioxide.

Sunlight

Bubbles of oxygen

CO_2

CO_2

Day time

O_2

Night time

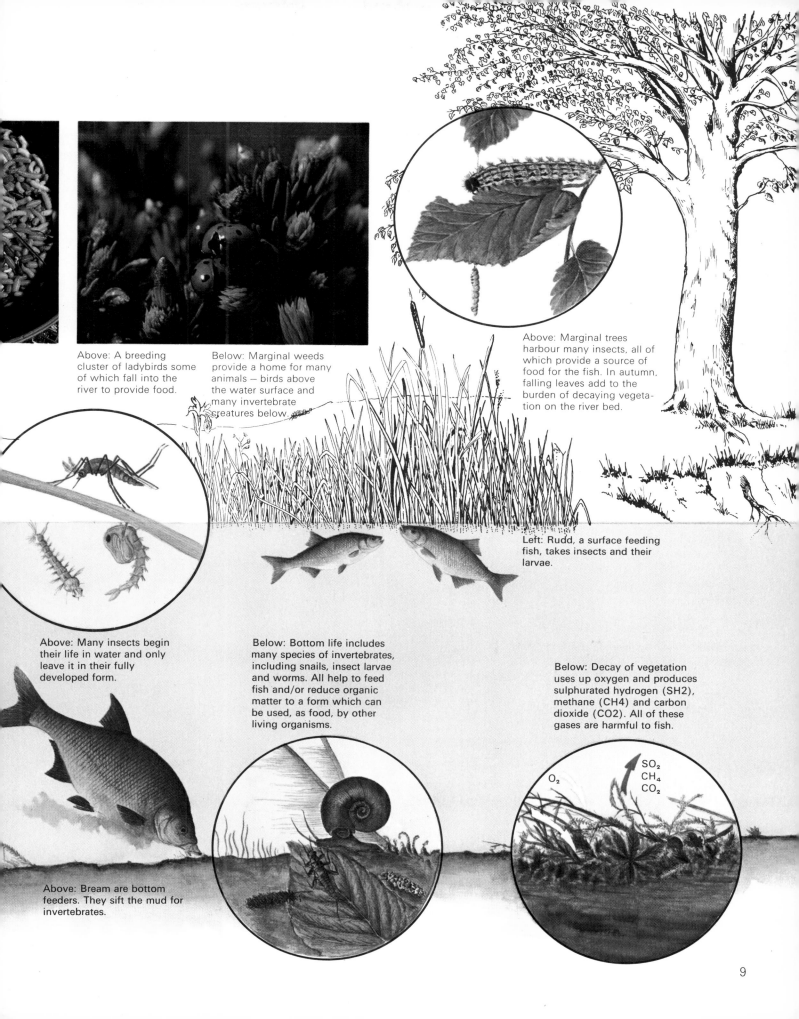

Above: A breeding cluster of ladybirds some of which fall into the river to provide food.

Below: Marginal weeds provide a home for many animals – birds above the water surface and many invertebrate creatures below.

Above: Marginal trees harbour many insects, all of which provide a source of food for the fish. In autumn, falling leaves add to the burden of decaying vegetation on the river bed.

Left: Rudd, a surface feeding fish, takes insects and their larvae.

Above: Many insects begin their life in water and only leave it in their fully developed form.

Below: Bottom life includes many species of invertebrates, including snails, insect larvae and worms. All help to feed fish and/or reduce organic matter to a form which can be used, as food, by other living organisms.

Below: Decay of vegetation uses up oxygen and produces sulphurated hydrogen (SH_2), methane (CH_4) and carbon dioxide (CO_2). All of these gases are harmful to fish.

Above: Bream are bottom feeders. They sift the mud for invertebrates.

O_2

SO_2
CH_4
CO_2

Fish of the rivers

All our freshwater fishes have bony skeletons. Most of them also have well-defined scale patterns. Sometimes the fish have hard scales although a few have extremely soft scales. Often the scales are so small that we think the fish has a smooth skin similar to our own. The position of the fish's fins, which can vary considerably from species to species, the type of its scales and shape of its body are the identifying features that enable us to give the fish common names. Scientists have given all fish Latin names which allow the different species to be identified anywhere in the world.

Fish do not breed like land animals and birds. Eggs are shed into the water by the female or hen fish and these are fertilized by the male, or cock fish. With few exceptions the eggs are released haphazardly with little thought of parental care. The stickleback does build a nest and the male fish spends time guarding the eggs until they hatch. Salmon and trout bury their eggs. The female scrapes a nest or redd with her tail and the eggs are shed into this nest. The male fertilizes the eggs which are then covered with gravel to prevent other species from eating them.

The European freshwater eel is exceptional in that it does not spawn in freshwater. In fact, it does not breed in Europe at all. When they are fully grown both male and female eels travel down the rivers to salt water. They then spend a year or more on the long and dangerous journey to the Sargasso Sea, which is in the South Atlantic. There they shed their eggs. After hatching, the tiny leaf-like creatures begin the long journey to the freshwater rivers. This takes them about three years and during the journey they change into elvers, resembling their parents, before they enter freshwater to begin the eel life cycle again.

Eels are said to spawn or breed only once in their lives. Our other freshwater fish species breed once every year when they are fully mature, although once again one species differs from the rest. The salmon hatches high up in the Highland rivers, spends a number of years as a parr growing all the time until it decides to head for the sea. The young salmon, which is known to anglers as a smolt, changes colour as it matures, adopting a silvery uniform. It spends its adult life feeding in the rich waters of the Arctic seas before returning to the river in which it began its life. The salmon does not spawn each year and it may only stay for two years in the sea before coming to the rivers.

CHUB

Leuciscus cephalus
Right: The chub is found in England and part of Scotland but is absent from Ireland. A thick-bodied fish that will take most baits.

ROACH

Rutilus rutilus
Below: A very common silver fish that is found in both still and flowing waters. The roach has a fine reputation among anglers as a fighter.

NASE

Chondrostoma nasus
(European species)
Below: A chub-like fish with a blunt nose. The nase lives in the deepwater parts of a river where there is a constant flow to the current. This fish feeds on minute larvae and the algae found on the river bed.

However, many fish spend up to five years in the sea and become very large. After spawning, quite a lot of salmon – called kelts at this stage – die but many will return to the sea to begin the feeding cycle over again.

There is an element of cross-breeding among the freshwater species. Rudd will spawn at the same time and in the same places as bream. The fish that result look a bit like both parents. The hybrid fish – which is the name we give to these cross-breeds – is often difficult to recognize. It may be the same size and shape

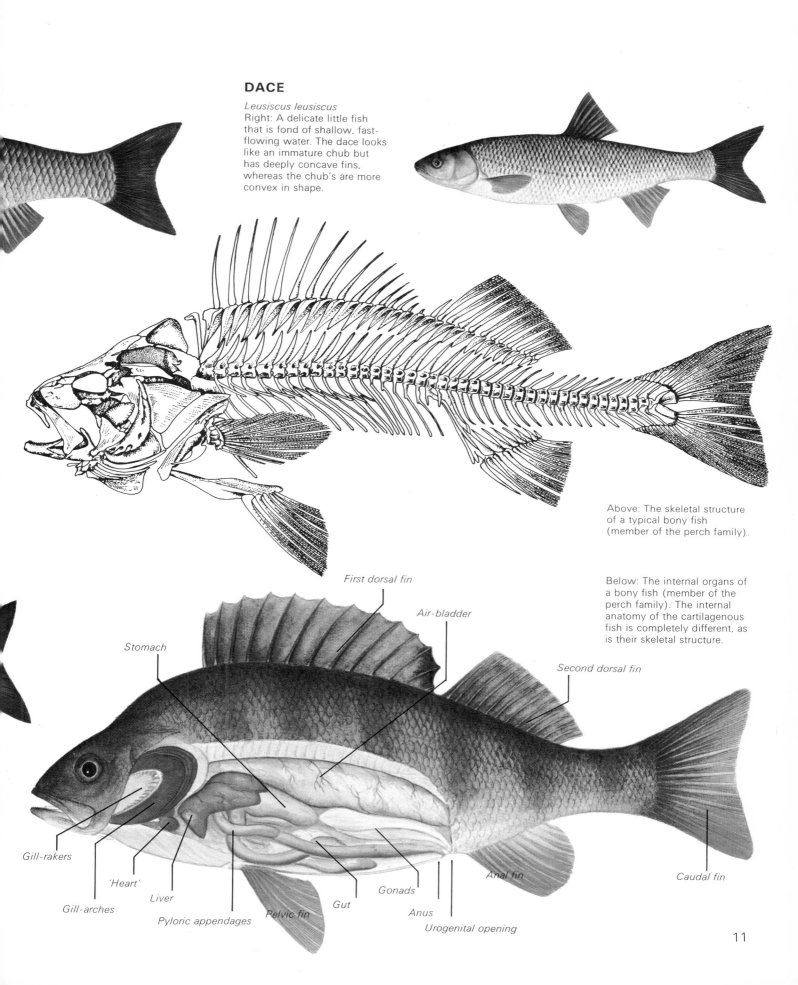

DACE

Leusiscus leusiscus
Right: A delicate little fish that is fond of shallow, fast-flowing water. The dace looks like an immature chub but has deeply concave fins, whereas the chub's are more convex in shape.

Above: The skeletal structure of a typical bony fish (member of the perch family).

Below: The internal organs of a bony fish (member of the perch family). The internal anatomy of the cartilagenous fish is completely different, as is their skeletal structure.

First dorsal fin

Air-bladder

Second dorsal fin

Stomach

Gill-rakers

'Heart'

Liver

Gill-arches

Pyloric appendages

Pelvic fin

Gut

Gonads

Anus

Urogenital opening

Anal fin

Caudal fin

River fish, big and small

as one parent but it might have a watered-down version of the other parent's colouring.

Fish grow throughout their lives. The size they eventually reach is directly related to the supply of food in the water in which they live. The more food there is in the water, the more the fish will eat and the larger they will become.

Not all Europe's freshwater fish are big. But, large or small, they all have a part to play in nature's plan. Essentially, the small fry form part of a food chain. They eat the tiny plankton creatures, deriving their food requirements from organisms so small that they are of little food value to bigger fish. Then the small fry are in turn eaten by the bigger fellows who live in the same waters.

Plankton – the microscopic life that drifts in the water – is a rich form of protein. Providing a water is free from pollution, this food source allows all our water-living creatures to get a healthy start in life. The barbel, a member of the carp family, will begin life eating plankton. When several centimetres long, the barbel begins to grub around at the bottom of the river for worms and invertebrates. (These are small creatures without backbones.) The four barbules around its mouth help the barbel to detect its food supplies. The gudgeon, loach and the mighty carp also have barbules which they, too, use as organs of detection in the constant hunt for food.

Our freshwater fish have different social habits. The pike and salmon are lonely fish. We rarely find them in groups, except at breeding times. Pike are predators so are avoided by other fish, including smaller pike. Salmon seek to lie in the best positions in the river. They like places where they will expend little energy and where they will be safe from the bigger fish as they wait for the urge to travel to the river's headwaters to breed. Salmon only rarely lie in shoals.

Many of the European freshwater species are shoal fish. This means that they choose to live together in numbers. The shoals mostly contain fish of an average size. This habit of forming shoals can affect our fishing. If we, as anglers, hook a bream as the shoal feeds around our baits, it becomes vitally important that we play the bream away from the feeding shoal before the hooked fish is able to communicate fear to the rest of the fish. We can throw in small amounts of groundbait upstream, followed by a baited hook, outside the feeding area to lure fish away from the shoal.

12

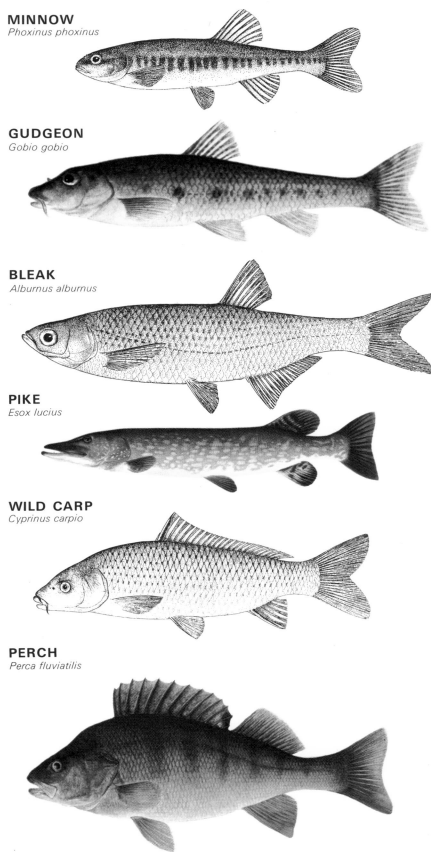

MINNOW
Phoxinus phoxinus

GUDGEON
Gobio gobio

BLEAK
Alburnus alburnus

PIKE
Esox lucius

WILD CARP
Cyprinus carpio

PERCH
Perca fluviatilis

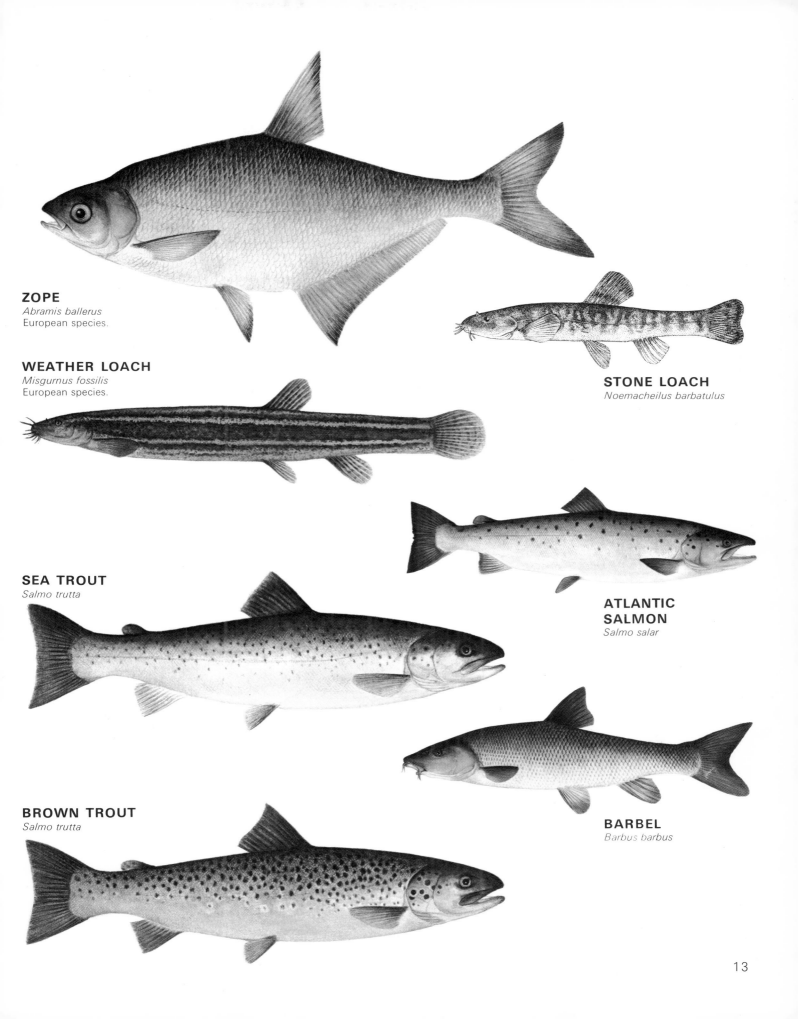

ZOPE
Abramis ballerus
European species.

WEATHER LOACH
Misgurnus fossilis
European species.

STONE LOACH
Noemacheilus barbatulus

SEA TROUT
Salmo trutta

**ATLANTIC
SALMON**
Salmo salar

BROWN TROUT
Salmo trutta

BARBEL
Barbus barbus

13

Fishing tackle

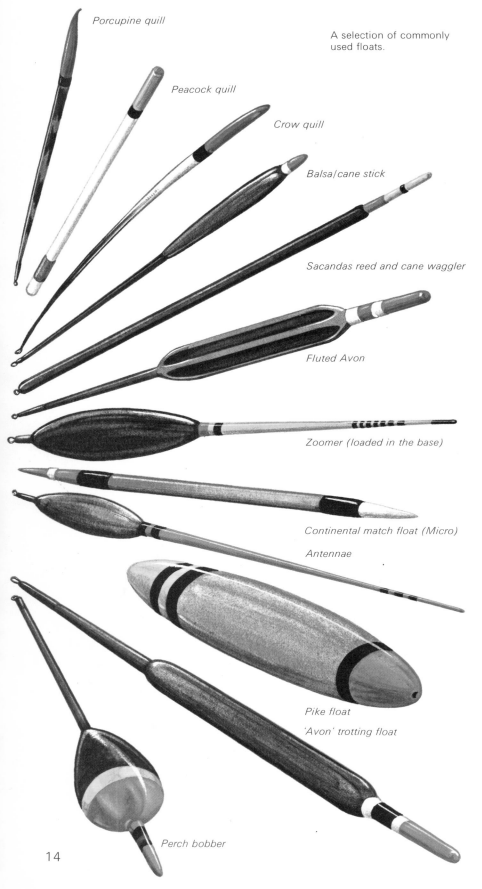

A selection of commonly used floats.

Porcupine quill

Peacock quill

Crow quill

Balsa/cane stick

Sacandas reed and cane waggler

Fluted Avon

Zoomer (loaded in the base)

Continental match float (Micro)

Antennae

Pike float

'Avon' trotting float

Perch bobber

The simplest form of fishing tackle is a hook, a length of cane or stick and a length of fine thread to connect the two. Although we use many more devices than this today the basic methods remain the same. Fishing is the art of luring a fish into accepting food that may not be natural to it and in such a way that its suspicions are not aroused. Modern rods give us the maximum fish-catching possibilities while retaining the maximum sensitivity to those vibrations that cause us to follow the sport. Fishing is hooking, feeling the movement of the quarry as it fights to escape, and then landing the hooked fish successfully.

Rods are designed to meet special needs. Spinning rods are made to cast a variety of different weights accurately over a distance. Float rods must feel light in the hand and yet they must also be responsive when playing a fish. Leger rods are made to cast weighted baits to fish that are generally larger than those taken on float tackle. Hollow fibre glass tubes form the basis of our rods today. Some rods are still formed from split bamboo cane but most future rods will use glass-reinforced plastic, known as GRP.

Practically all anglers use nylon monofilament fishing lines in fresh water. These are cheap and strong and will last for a full angling season. You should try to balance the power of your rod in relation to the line so that a strike will not break the nylon. For general river fishing a 11- or 12-foot float rod will handle lines of $2\frac{1}{2}$–$4\frac{1}{2}$ lb B.S. or breaking strain. Most leger rods would call for a line of at least $3\frac{1}{2}$–6 lb B.S.

Two kinds of reel are used by float and leger anglers. The older, and now less favoured, reel is the centre pin. Casting with the centre pin is difficult because the spool will not spin easily to let the line flow off and the line has to be pulled off to flick cast the float. However, the fixed spool reel makes casting easy for a beginner. This relies on having a stationary spool around which the nylon is wrapped by a bale arm. Casts are made by opening the bale arm. The handle of the reel is then wound slightly so that the bale arm is automatically engaged. Fixed spool reels also have a slipping clutch device that lets the line pull off the spool at a pre-set friction rate when a large fish pulls more strongly than was expected. This is helpful to the beginner but it is far better that he should learn to use the curve of his rod when he has to subdue the big fish.

Three correct rings for a coarse fishing rod.

Low profile ring suitable for all leger rods.

High profile ring for float rods, the ring stands off from the rod blank preventing wet lines sticking, so cutting down the distance cast.

A float rod tip ring with jewelled centre. The shank is internally threaded to accommodate swing and quivertips, used when legering with the rod.

Below: Leads used by the coarse fisherman.

Catherine lead

Drilled bullet lead

Split shot

Barrel lead

Styl lead

'Mouse Dropping'

Above: The simplest form of connection between fixed line and roach pole rod uses an elastic shock absorbing section to prevent breaks on the strike.

Left: Rods for fishing on rivers and streams —
A: A 12-ft float rod with corked handle and high profile rings. This type of rod will give the greatest control over your float and fish.
B. A roach pole is fished with a tight line to the rod tip so has no winch fittings for a reel. Poles can be of any length — 22-ft rods are not unusual.
C. A standard 10-ft leger rod used for river species, chub, barbel and bream, as well as carp and other stillwater species.
D. Spinning rods vary in length depending on the species and size of river fished; an 8-ft rod will cope with most situations.
E. Telescopic rods are coming into fashion. They may well be useful for the fisher who wants to keep a rod in the boot of his car.

Below: The coarse fisherman's reels:

A   B   C   D   E

Below: A closed-face fixed spool reel, the ABU 505.

Below: The Mitchell 300 is an open-faced fixed spool reel.

Below: A fine trotting reel, the centre-pin.

The roach

The roach is probably the most popular of coarse fish, not just because it can be found in most waters, but because great care and skill are needed to catch one. A big roach is a prize indeed, but even a 6 in specimen from a polluted canal may rank as a prize catch with a 2 lb plus fish from a clean river.

For many anglers the word fishing means, quite simply, roach fishing. The fish has a grip on the interest of most anglers which ensures that it is fished for throughout the season, but the late winter is a favourite period since the banks are clean and the roach shoals are localized. The fish is tolerant of pollution, it will stand overcrowding and while it will grow large in a favourable environment, it appears to thrive as a stunted dwarf in the smallest of farm ponds.

A technique known as "long trotting" is one of the most interesting methods of roach fishing. This means allowing the bait to run through the swim at the speed of the current but holding it back every few yards. This makes the bait rise in the water and often entices the roach to take the hook. Good baits for this form of fishing include maggots, the chrysalis of the maggot – sometimes called a caster – and bread flake.

The float should be placed on the line at exactly the depth of the water and should be fixed at both the top and the bottom. In fast water a larger float is needed than for slower runs. This is because more weight, such as lead shot, is required to make sure the bait is well down towards the bottom where the fish are usually feeding.

Long trotting may be carried out with a fixed spool reel but the best reel for the job is the centre pin (see page 15). With a centre pin the float will run through without too much variation from the speed of the current. Since the fish will sometimes be feeding a long way downstream it is a good idea to have a rod which will bend throughout its whole length so that the fine line does not break when you strike.

Make certain the roach are waiting to take your bait by feeding samples of your hook bait into the swim in balls of groundbait.

Sometimes it is not possible to trot the bait for a long way because there are other anglers downstream. In this case you can catch your roach by a method known as "swimming the stream". Fix the float top and bottom again and set it at the depth of the water. Cast directly in front of you and allow the bait to

run through but not as far as in trotting. This is a good method to use with a roach pole. No reel is used and there is just a short length of line between the pole tip and the float.

There are times when the fish will not take moving baits. Winter is the most obvious example. "Laying on" is one method to use at this time. Set the float higher up the line so that the bait and perhaps one shot will lie on the bottom. If you fish one spot for a time and then lift the rod and let some line out before holding back again, you are using a method known as "stret-pegging". This means that the bait is swept across the bottom in an arc. You can search an area in this way. This technique works well in coloured water conditions when the bait might be yellow maggot, small red worms or the tail of a lob worm. The bite is usually shown very well when using the float but this may not be so when you take your roach by the method known as "legering". In this method the bait is laid hard on the bottom and a float will probably not be used. One way to tell when the roach is taking the bait is to use a fine tip to the rod. It is called a quiver tip. The bait may be held on the bottom by a drilled bullet but it is important to remember to use the lightest weight which will hold bottom.

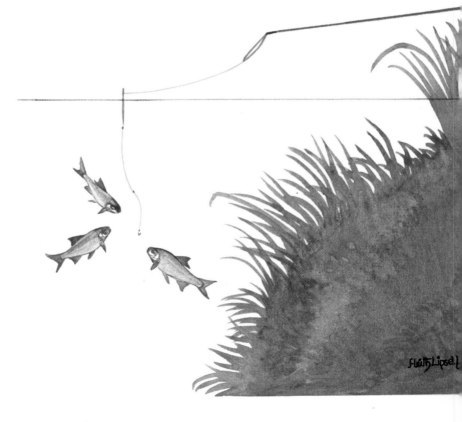

Below: Pole fishing under the rod tip using a fixed length of line which has an elastic shock absorber connection between tip and nylon. The float is dropped onto the water to be followed downstream by the rod tip.

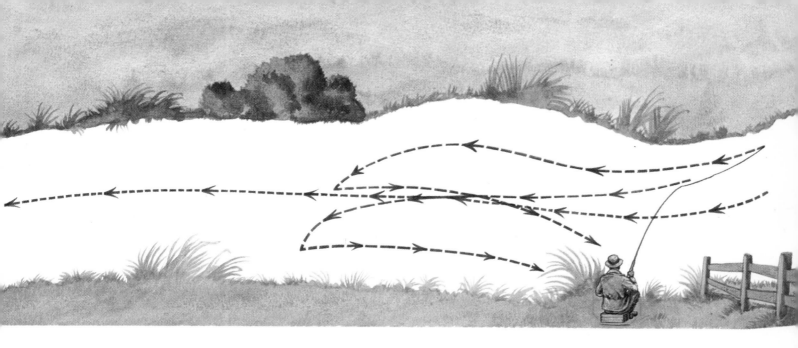

Left: This is the way to find the depth of the stream in front of you. Set up your tackle, rod, reel, float and hook. Estimate the depth of water, then set the float at that depth. Fix the plummet lead to the hook, swing the tackle out onto the surface watching the float carefully. If pulled under the float has been set too shallow; too deep will be shown by the float falling on the water. The correct setting is when only the float tip shows.

Above: Swimming the stream (arrowed in red) is a method for fishing every bit of the available river, in front of the angler's pitch. The float is cast across and slightly upstream. It is followed, in an arc, by the rod tip. After retrieval a shorter cast is made to cover water closer in to the angler. Long trotting (arrowed in blue) is a method where the bait is allowed to swim down the river, at the speed of the current, fishing at distance so covering a lot of water.

Below: Left to right — long trotting with bait tripping the river bed. Arresting the float's travel will cause the bait to rise in the water enticing fish into taking the offering. Laying on is a way of tethering a bait hard on the bottom with a tight line between float and shots lying on the river bed. A simple leger rig uses a split shot to stop the bullet leger weight.

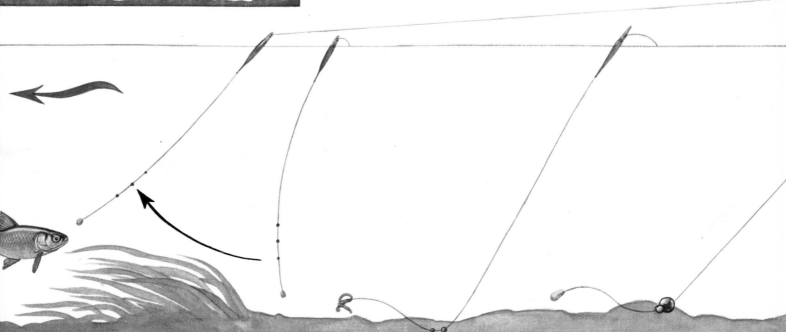

Chub and dace

The chub and dace are two fish which are sometimes caught in the same swim. In the early summer both these fish will be found swimming on rippling water, which is usually quite shallow. For the dace this is his home throughout most of the year but the chub usually moves to slower water by the middle of July. The fully grown dace is a much smaller fish than the chub and has different habits. It is much more active than the chub, moving swiftly to feed on insects. Old time anglers knew this and sometimes called the fish the dart.

Dace fishing is good fun. It is best to use fine tackle and to take the fish by long trotting (see page 16) or swimming the stream. Use a light 11 or 12 foot long rod with a centre pin reel loaded with a nylon line of about $2\frac{1}{2}$ lb breaking strain. A good float to use is one with a balsa top and a wire stem at the bottom. These ride the swift water well without being pulled about too much by the currents. The hook should be small and a size 16 is the ideal. Bait for the dace may be maggot, caster and, in water which is a little coloured, a single red worm.

Catch the dace by throwing in to the water a few maggots or casters and then casting in at once. This means that your bait is following the samples very closely. The bite, when it comes, is swift and you should strike at the smallest movement of the float. The speed of the dace – and the fact that it feeds near the surface – tempts experienced anglers to catch the fish on an artificial fly, using a fly fishing rod and line.

The chub is a very different fish but he, too, may be taken on the fly. The chub can be caught on more baits than any other fish. The chub can be a big fish and your tackle strength should be built up to match its size.

Use an Avon-style rod. This has plenty of bend. It is named after the River Avon in Hampshire, England, famous for big chub.

The line should be not less than 3 lb breaking strain. Hook size may vary from a size 16 when using single maggot bait, right through to a size 6 when using lumps of cheese. The chub is one of the greediest of fish but he is also extremely shy. Make one false move, such as

---

Right: The tucked half-blood knot is best when joining eyed hooks to nylon. Make five turns of nylon around the main line after attaching the hook. Take the free end of the line through the first loop, at the hook eye, then pass the nylon back through the larger loop formed. Wet the line to lubricate the coils and pull up tight.

A spade-end hook, whipping knot for attaching nylon droppers.

1. Form a loop in the nylon line.

2. Trapping the hook bend and nylon loop between your fingers, begin to bind the free end of the nylon around the hook shank.

3. Try to keep the bindings fairly tight and close together.

4. After taking the nylon around the hook shank at least four times, pass the free end of the nylon through the loop of nylon at the hook bend.

5. Take up the knot tight by pulling on the main line, then clip off the tag end to make the knot neat in presentation.

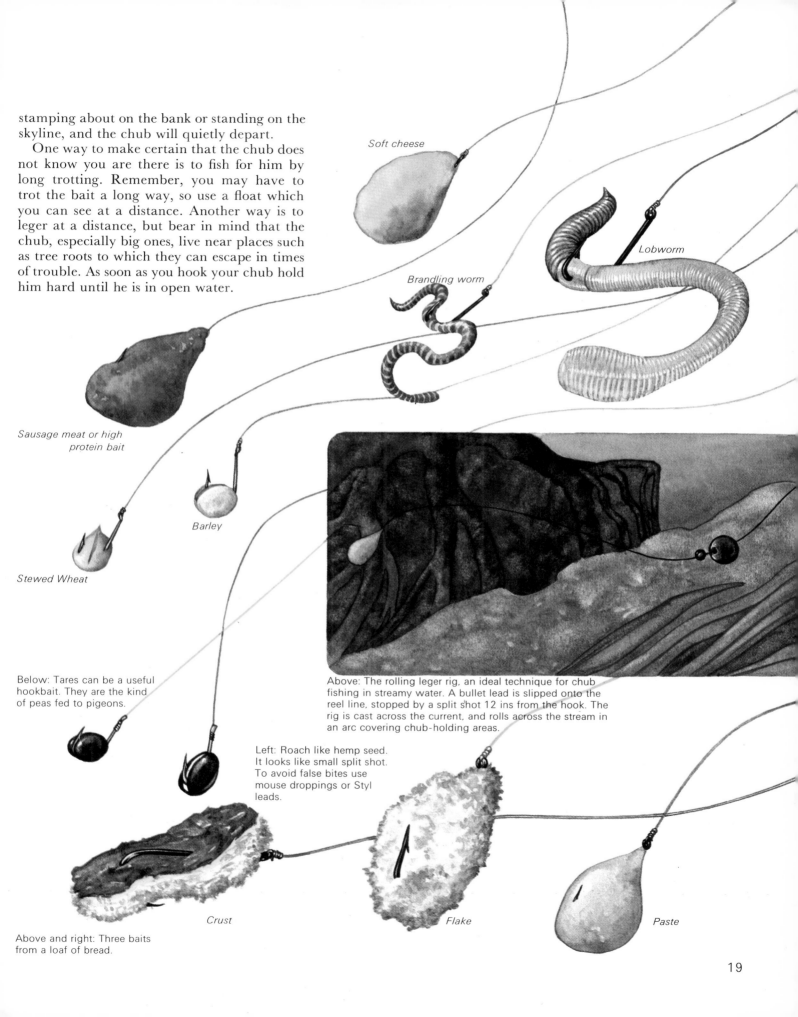

stamping about on the bank or standing on the skyline, and the chub will quietly depart.

One way to make certain that the chub does not know you are there is to fish for him by long trotting. Remember, you may have to trot the bait a long way, so use a float which you can see at a distance. Another way is to leger at a distance, but bear in mind that the chub, especially big ones, live near places such as tree roots to which they can escape in times of trouble. As soon as you hook your chub hold him hard until he is in open water.

Soft cheese

Lobworm

Brandling worm

Sausage meat or high protein bait

Barley

Stewed Wheat

Below: Tares can be a useful hookbait. They are the kind of peas fed to pigeons.

Above: The rolling leger rig, an ideal technique for chub fishing in streamy water. A bullet lead is slipped onto the reel line, stopped by a split shot 12 ins from the hook. The rig is cast across the current, and rolls across the stream in an arc covering chub-holding areas.

Left: Roach like hemp seed. It looks like small split shot. To avoid false bites use mouse droppings or Styl leads.

Crust

Flake

Paste

Above and right: Three baits from a loaf of bread.

Barbel, bleak and gudgeon

Many fish and especially the chub will take baits other than maggots.

Cheese: try using Edam cheese which has been cut into small cubes, placed in a bowl and covered for about 20 seconds with hot water.

Meat baits: luncheon meat is a good bait for chub and barbel. Cut it into cubes at home and take it to the water in a clean cloth or a polythene bag.

Seed baits: these include wheat, hemp and tares. Place two or three cups of the bait into a saucepan and rinse well. Cover the bait with fresh water and bring it to the boil. Simmer it gently for about 20 minutes but avoid letting it get too mushy. Wheat should be fluffy, hemp and tares should be just split.

Another fish which may turn up when you have been groundbaiting for chub is the barbel. Since this fish is stronger than the chub you will need strong tackle to have a chance of landing one. Your line should not be less than $3\frac{1}{2}$ lb breaking strain. A hook within the 12 to 6 range is the best, since baits of varying types and size may then be used. The barbel almost always feeds on the bottom and this means that he may best be caught by using leger fishing tackle. Because the fish likes to root about on the river bed like a pig, special pieces of tackle have been developed to help to catch him.

The swim feeder is the most important of these aids. This consists of a clear plastic tube with a strip of lead along one side to take it to the bottom. You fill the tube with samples of the hookbait which the force of the water spreads in a trail just downstream of your baited hook. The swim feeder is fixed on the line about 12 inches above the hook and is kept from running down to the hook by a swivel or a split shot. Another way of getting the same effect is to use an ordinary running leger rig but to squeeze a ball of groundbait around the leger when casting out. Good baits for catching the barbel include maggots, worms and luncheon meat cut into half-inch squares. You may have to cast a long way to the place where the barbel are lying and it is a good idea to put a tiny stalk of grass across the bend of the hook to keep the luncheon meat on. The barbel fights strongly until it is netted. It is therefore important to make sure that the fish is rested before releasing it into a strong current.

A fish which looks very like the barbel is the gudgeon. But there is one big difference. The gudgeon does not grow much above 5 or 6 inches in length or more than a few ounces in

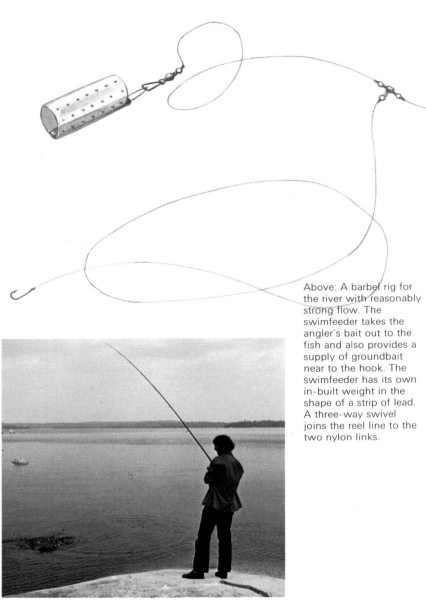

Above: A barbel rig for the river with reasonably strong flow. The swimfeeder takes the angler's bait out to the fish and also provides a supply of groundbait near to the hook. The swimfeeder has its own in-built weight in the shape of a strip of lead. A three-way swivel joins the reel line to the two nylon links.

Above: Spinning is a mobile sport. With a few lures in your pocket you are constantly on the move searching out where the fish are lying.

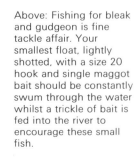

Above: Fishing for bleak and gudgeon is fine tackle affair. Your smallest float, lightly shotted, with a size 20 hook and single maggot bait should be constantly swum through the water whilst a trickle of bait is fed into the river to encourage these small fish.

weight. You can tell the difference between large gudgeon and small barbel by looking at their barbules. These are really taste organs which help the fish to find their food on the bottom. They look like moustaches and the gudgeon 'has two, while the barbel has four. The gudgeon should be fished for with very fine tackle. Make sure the size 16 hook with a single maggot or a tiny red worm is just tripping the bottom. The fish is often used by anglers as a bait for the predators such as pike, perch or zander.

This is also true of another small fish, the bleak, but the bleak has different habits. It spends its life in large shoals darting about at the water's surface where it feeds on insects. It is interesting to compare the shape of a bleak's head with that of a gudgeon. The under lip of the surface-feeding bleak juts out, while that of the bottom-feeding gudgeon is underslung like a vacuum cleaner. Catch your bleak by using a single maggot on a size 16 hook. The shot should be placed close to the float so that the bait falls slowly through the surface water where the bleak do most of their feeding.

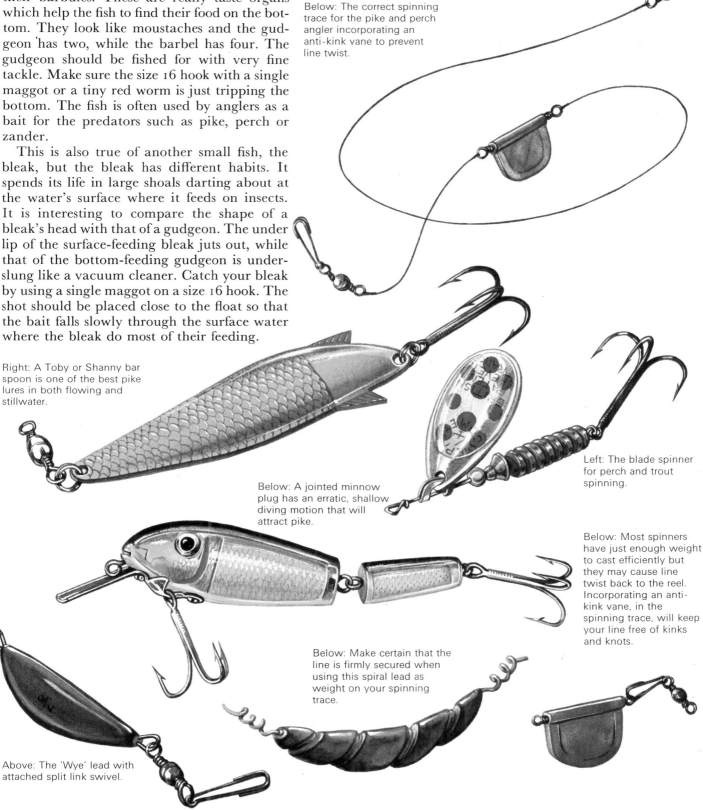

Below: The correct spinning trace for the pike and perch angler incorporating an anti-kink vane to prevent line twist.

Right: A Toby or Shanny bar spoon is one of the best pike lures in both flowing and stillwater.

Left: The blade spinner for perch and trout spinning.

Below: A jointed minnow plug has an erratic, shallow diving motion that will attract pike.

Below: Most spinners have just enough weight to cast efficiently but they may cause line twist back to the reel. Incorporating an anti-kink vane, in the spinning trace, will keep your line free of kinks and knots.

Below: Make certain that the line is firmly secured when using this spiral lead as weight on your spinning trace.

Above: The 'Wye' lead with attached split link swivel.

Fishing the small streams

There is fun to be had in fishing the very small streams which twist across the land. They often hold quite big fish and are the home of several different species. It is important to remember that small water fishing is usually close range work. This means that you must be particularly careful not to make a noise or to stand against the skyline. Remember some fish, such as the chub and the trout, grow big on the ample food which the over-grown banks of the little stream provide.

In most fishing a float has three jobs to do. It tells you when you have a bite. It places the bait in front of a fish and it helps you to control your tackle. Usually the first job is the most important but not in small stream fishing. This is because the fish you are after may be only a few feet away, although tucked in awkward corners under bushes. Small stream floats should be chosen so that they help to put the bait in front of the fish and to control your tackle. For instance, a small piece of cork, about as big as an oak apple, looks natural as it floats the few feet to the fish. Even more important, it is big enough to carry a bunch of maggots or wriggling red worms right into the fish-holding area. When you get a bite you can usually tell by watching the line, which will straighten out at a speed faster than that of the current. A *bubble float* made of clear plastic can be useful in these conditions. If you need extra weight to cast a little distance, the float may be half-filled with water. Most small streams zig-zag and fold their way towards larger rivers. This means that every few yards there is an inviting corner with deep, fish-holding water under the bank on which you are fishing.

Dapping is a good method of taking fish from these spots. Remove the float and crawl to the edge of the bank like a Red Indian stalking a buffalo. Only the tip of the rod should be pushed over the water and the bait lowered gently into the run. You can pinch a shot onto the line about 12 inches above the hook to provide a little added weight if required. Because they have a little weight in themselves, worms and grasshoppers make good baits for this style of fishing. This method is especially useful when the banks are lined with trees such as the alder. The chub, especially, like to patrol beneath the tree's branches snapping up any fallen "creepy-crawlies".

It is a mistake to use very fine line in this type of fishing. When you hook a fish it is not possible to play it in the usual manner and

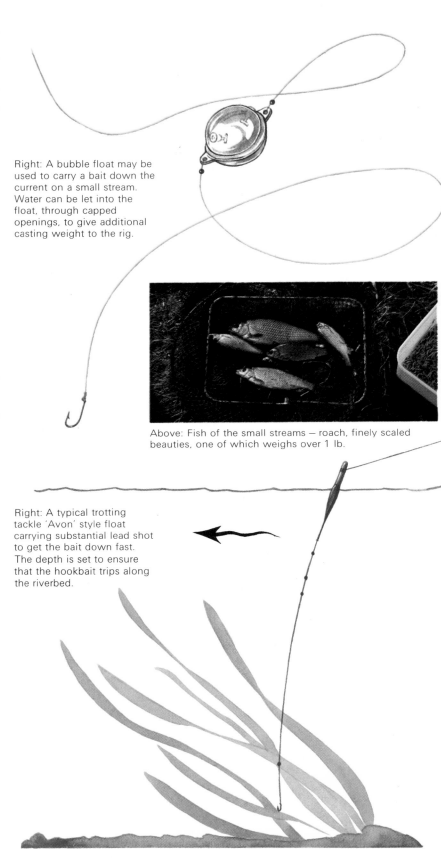

Right: A bubble float may be used to carry a bait down the current on a small stream. Water can be let into the float, through capped openings, to give additional casting weight to the rig.

Above: Fish of the small streams — roach, finely scaled beauties, one of which weighs over 1 lb.

Right: A typical trotting tackle 'Avon' style float carrying substantial lead shot to get the bait down fast. The depth is set to ensure that the hookbait trips along the riverbed.

22

you need a line and hook which enable you to hold the fish hard until you can slip a landing net under it. Use line of not less than $3\frac{1}{2}$ lb breaking strain and an eyed, tie on, hook. The best knot to stand the strain put upon the tackle is the tucked half-blood (see page 18). Half of the fun in this fishing is to try for a particular fish in a swim. Hours can slip away as you lower and raise the bait if the wrong fish moves towards it. Big fish are crafty. So remember, it's no use being impatient. If you are to land the fish of your choice it is often a matter of staying power. In short, to outwit the crafty "big one", you must be crafty, too.

The secret is to get to know your fish well. Study it thoroughly so that you come to know its ways and wiles. When you are up against a crafty old fish you will be able to outwit it.

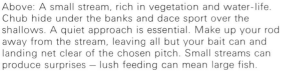

Above: A small stream, rich in vegetation and water-life. Chub hide under the banks and dace sport over the shallows. A quiet approach is essential. Make up your rod away from the stream, leaving all but your bait can and landing net clear of the chosen pitch. Small streams can produce surprises — lush feeding can mean large fish.

Below: Dapping is a most interesting form of angling. You can use a natural bait, like a grub, caterpillar or large insect on the hook. They will all take fish if presented in a lifelike fashion. Taking care to remain hidden from view, part the rushes carefully, poking the rod out to dap the bait onto the water surface.

Legering in the stream

Dapping is a method for the hazy, lazy, days of summer. The winter calls for other ways of taking fish. After the autumn gales and rains have cleared the leaves from the trees and flooded them away, the small stream looks very different. The shallow runs are open to the sky and do not hold the fish as they do in the summer. You will find that the chub, roach and dace have moved into the deeper holes which have been formed by the current at each bend in the stream. The whole pace of life in the colder water slows and the fish do not feed as often as they do in the summer months. They may still be taken by float fishing, but the winter is the ideal time for legering (see pages 16–17).

Small stream legering is a delicate affair. You do not need to cast far. The current is rarely strong enough to require heavy leads to hold the bottom of the stream. Tiny drilled bullets or single split shots (page 15) may be all that is needed. In some cases the weight of the bait itself will do the trick. One way to fish the leger is to use the strength of the current to roll the bait into the fish-holding areas. You do this by casting across and slightly downstream. If you hold the rod tip high you will find that the bait will be trundled into the deep hole.

The bite may be signalled by the stopping of the movement of the leger or by an unusual movement of the line. If there is no immediate bite you should wait until the bait comes to rest. Wind the reel very gently until the line is almost tight to the weight. If you then hold the line between your finger and thumb, just above the rod handle, every tiny pluck at the bait will be felt. A definite pull should be answered by a lifting of the rod tip so that the fish will be hooked.

Sometimes it is not possible to fish downstream because of bankside obstructions. Legering upstream is just as effective. You should cast into the tail of the run and tighten gently when the bait comes to rest. The bite, when it comes, may be shown by a loosening of the line, a bowing, as the fish picks up the bait and the current puts pressure on the line. Another way to use the leger is to adopt the dapping method. You simply poke the rod tip only over the bank and lower the bait into the swim. There is usually no problem with bite detection when you fish like this as you are so close to the fish. Sometimes you need to persuade the fish to feed by groundbaiting. This is the name we

Left: Fishing the weightless bait. A small lobworm is hooked, then flicked out across and slightly downstream. Allow the current to trundle the bait round into the area you hope holds fish. Wind in any slack line until you feel a slight resistance to the rod tip. You will now have a positive contact between rod and worm, bites can be detected by holding the line between your fingers feeling for gentle plucking tremors.

Below: Three types of swimfeeder. A. Conical feeder with legered line running through the centre of the feeder. It is ideal for maggot feeding in fairly strong water. B. The open-end swimfeeder can be used to deposit groundbait, or a combination of maggots and groundbait on beds of rivers or lakes. To hold maggots, during the cast, the ends of the feeder are plugged with stiff groundbait which will disperse when in the water releasing the grubs. C. A small block-end feeder is suitable for feeding a swim with grubs. The hook link runs through a swivel, stopped with a split shot. A swimfeeder is an accurate method of placing a hookbait within your groundbaited area. Loose feeding when fishing at distance can never be as accurate.

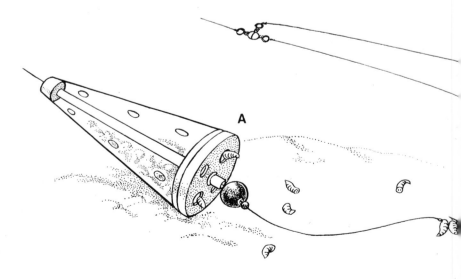

A

Above: The Overhead Cast. Open the bale arm on the reel picking up the line on the finger.

Above: Take the rod back over your shoulder, trying to keep it as upright as possible.

Above: Begin the forward cast from this position. Power to cast comes from both arms.

Above: Bring the rod smartly forward following the trajectory of the float with your eyes.

Above: Stop the distance of the cast by jamming your finger down onto the rim of the spool.

give to throwing samples of the hookbait into the swim.

In small stream groundbaiting it is important to remember that too much groundbait is not a good thing. If the bait you are using is maggot then a few every so often is a good idea. If bread flake is the hookbait then a small amount of ground-up bread crumbs will be right. If worm is the hookbait then you should throw in just a few chopped up worms. Remember, though, not too much. The ideal is "a little and often" and this is a principle which will work for most types of fishing. Small stream fishing means plenty of movement. When you take a good fish from a swim which is only a yard deep the others soon depart.

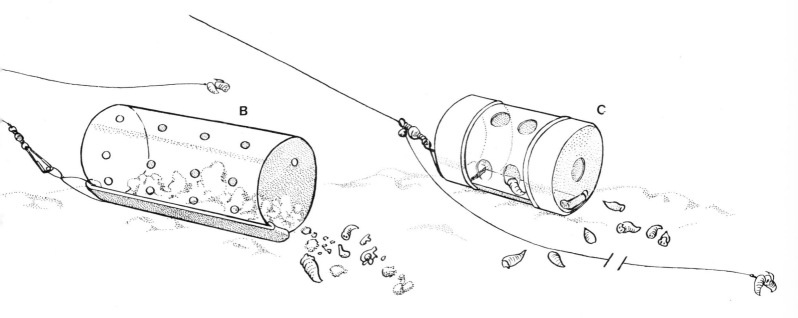

Canals: fisheries of the future?

Canals are artificial waterways designed to enable the movement of barges across countries. Many of the canals, in the British Isles, were built before the year 1800 when they proved the cheapest method of carrying manufactured goods in bulk. At the same time the canals carried water, used to irrigate agricultural land. They could also be used to remove water, as part of the land drainage system.

Of the 5000 miles of canal in Britain, at the time of the Industrial Revolution, only about 1500 miles remain open to navigation. A concerted effort is now being made to keep these remaining miles of canal open for both recreational and barge traffic. The canal system can offer good fishing possibilities, especially as boat traffic along the canals moves the water. The passage of boats creates a rejuvenating force by shifting from the bottom the silt that would otherwise settle and smother the bottom-growing waterweed. This cleansing action is important when we consider that most canals have an average depth of only 3 ft 3 ins, which could soon become heavily silted with soil blown from the land mass. Excessive weed is cut regularly, although there are canal bodies using chemical control methods that may prove to have a detrimental effect on fish and other water-living life forms.

Canals are not true stillwaters, although at times it is difficult to see any movement of the water. With the passage of a boat along the waterway, a certain amount of water travels with the barge. As the boat passes through a lock in a downward direction water escapes through the lock. This water is replaced at a high point on the canal. It is pumped, through a system of feeder channels, from a holding reservoir. All this movement of water is good for fishing.

The canal gives three possible fisheries to an angler. First, the reservoir that could be a trout fishery or stillwater coarse fishing lake. Then the carrier channels, though small, can provide running water fishing for some of the smaller species. When rivers are used in the topping-up process, there are even better prospects. Lastly, the canal itself brings fishing to places where a normal river could not flow because some canals cross hilly ground via a lock arrangement. Another bonus is that the canals pass through, or end in, city centres bringing fishing to the hearts of areas with huge populations.

We must guard our canals jealously and if possible improve them. Various angling clubs

Above: After unhooking a fish, lower it gently into the keepnet. Dropping it into the net may injure it and frighten others that are in your swim.
Left: Don't grasp a fish too tightly when removing the hook. Like any small creature fish have feelings. Too much handling will also remove scales and the protective slime from the fish's body.
Below: Never be afraid to ask questions when you are learning, but do not create a disturbance by moving about on the skyline or stamping your feet. Keep still and learn by watching the angler's every move.

Above: Fish will feed in two main places within the canal: on shelves that are formed by the passage of boats, where a prolific growth of surface and bankside water weeds supports snails and other small creatures, and at the bottom of the canal where there are weeds of a different kind, within which fish find the aquatic forms of fly life, eggs and small fish. Try both depths and remember that your arrival may send fish across to the shelter of the far bank. They can be reached, even when fishing light tackle, by using a zoomer or loaded float to carry the bait and float across to them.

have leased the fishing rights to British canals from the British Waterways Board, but in most cases a day fishing permit can be had from the controlling club. Remember that a fishing licence is also necessary. Maps and a booklet on the canals are published by the Waterways Board who also give much helpful printed information.

When the British canals were created in the last quarter of the eighteenth century they introduced long stretches of water into areas of the countryside which had previously lacked any really reasonable lengths. These canals brought about changes in the plant and bird life of these regions and today fishermen have reason to be grateful to the canal pioneers since many of the canals offer splendid fishing opportunities.

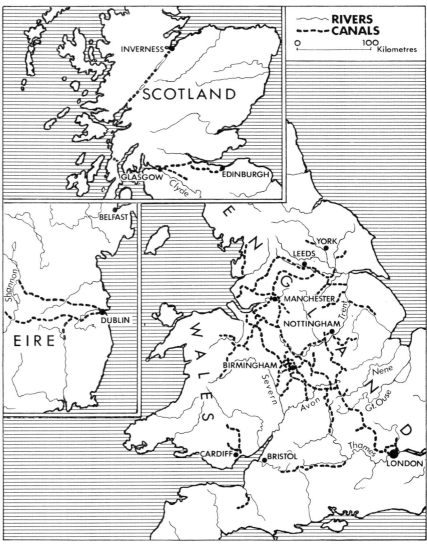

Fishing the canals

Fishing the canals may be very like fishing in small streams. This is because some canal systems hold large fish and you are almost always fishing at close range. The big difference is that on a small stream you can move on when you frighten the fish, whereas on the canal there will be other anglers on the towpath. Pleasure boats can also complicate canal fishing and there may be no bankside cover from which to fish. This means that even where you expect to catch large fish such as the tench you may have to use fine tackle. The fish are shy and will not tolerate the towpath vibrations, boat disturbance and bait delivered on coarse tackle.

Use a line of 2 lb breaking strain with a hook link down to 1 lb. The hook should be small, probably not larger than a size 16 and down to a size 20. Floats, too, should be delicate and there are some special types for canal work. Remember that canal fishing is like angling in the land of Lilliput. You, as Gulliver, must be as careful as you can to fit into the picture. This means that when you groundbait you should do so with great care and use very small amounts.

One of the ways to beat the bankside vibrations caused by some of the other "giants" on the towpath is to fish on the far side of the canal. This is where some of the special floats come into use. These are called darts and they have a loaded base to take the finely balanced rig through the air to the far bank. They also allow for a slow-falling bait – shotting pattern. These floats should be fixed at the bottom only, with a shot on each side of the bottom ring. One of these shots may be quite large. This means that only small shots are used between the float and the hook so that the bait tumbles slowly towards the bottom.

Sometimes you will find there is a decided drift along the length of the canal. The dart is a good float to use at this time because you cast out and then sink the tip of the rod below the surface. A turn or two of the reel handle will ensure that the line is buried below the surface drifting water. It is possible to use the drifting state of the canal to help you to take fish. This is called "swimming the stream" in miniature. Good tackle for this is a pole fishing rig. Use line of the same breaking strain as on the reel fishing gear but change the float to one of the specials developed on the Continent for use with the pole. These have a fine tip and are very sensitive. Set the bait to trip the bottom or

just above it. This is because many canals have a fine, silty, bed and if fished over depth the bait may be buried. Most canals hold roach, bream, tench, gudgeon and perch. Some have carp and pike as well and if you have been catching fish – and have been careful not to frighten them away – you should suspect their presence if the bites stop. The most important thing to remember when fishing the canals is noise control. If you obey the following rules you will not frighten the fish.

1. Never clump along the path.
2. Do not drop your basket with a thump.
3. It is not a good idea to hammer the rod rest into the bank.
4. You really must be quiet.

Right: Mike Prichard, stretching the net to a common bream, on The Grand Canal at Prosperous, Co. Kildare, Ireland. This canal is one of the best for canal catches in the whole of Europe.

Far right: Rudd, common bream and hybrids (between the two species), figure in a catch from the Grand Canal.

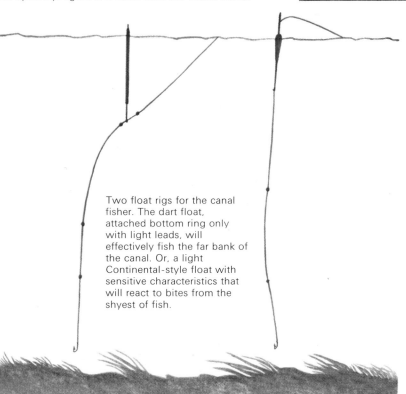

Two float rigs for the canal fisher. The dart float, attached bottom ring only with light leads, will effectively fish the far bank of the canal. Or, a light Continental-style float with sensitive characteristics that will react to bites from the shyest of fish.

Below: The nylon link-leger is a simple rig. Fold a slip of nylon over the reel line, then pinch on just enough shot to hold bottom. Stop the leger slipping down to the hook with a small stop shot. Don't pinch the leger shots on too tightly. If the rig gets fast in underwater obstructions, a pull will slide the leger shots off the link to free the hook.

A balsa/cane stick float.

A 'Boréal' float, used in France.

The 'Micro' continental match float.

A porcupine quill.

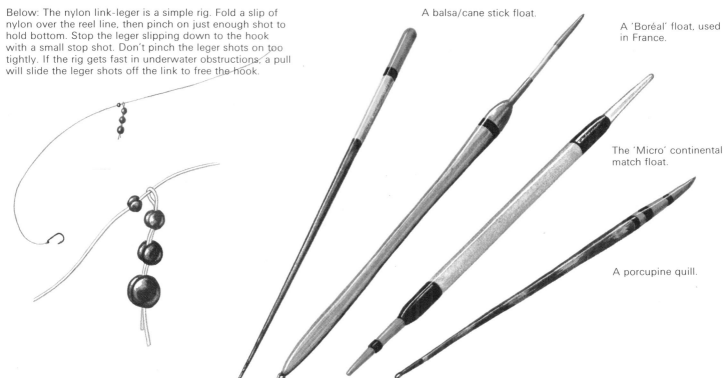

Above: A selection of useful canal-fishing floats.

Stillwaters: lake, pond and pool

Stillwaters come in many shapes and sizes, from the vastness of the Irish loughs and the deep, inky black waters of the lochs of Scotland, to the lakes and ponds of the lowlands of East Anglia and the coastal belt of Europe. Even the tiniest of stillwaters, the farm pool, takes its place with the large expanses of freshwater in providing a living place for fish. They all have one thing in common. They are able to support life without the strength and obvious food-bringing properties of a river. True, some have feeder streams but the stillwater is essentially self-contained.

The fish that live in our lakes, ponds, or pools may be exactly the same species that we find in the running waters. With few exceptions, fish can adapt to living where there are no current flows or other aids to oxygenate the water. Of course this capacity to adapt to life in stillwater has not happened overnight. But there are some fish – trout, chub and even salmon, for example – that man has successfully "seeded" into stillwaters in the last century. These species were quick to make themselves at home. Often a species such as rainbow trout has been brought vast distances to provide sport and food in a new country. We have sent the brown trout from Britain to New Zealand where it thrives, growing larger than it does in European waters.

The freshwater eel, spawned in the Sargasso Sea, will eventually pass up the rivers through tiny streamlets, to make its way into stillwaters to live and to grow to breeding size.

One thing is certain. Stillwaters do not fish in quite the same way throughout the year as the running water fisheries. In the lakes of the cold, northerly lands, trout are slow to respond in winter to the angler's lure. In more southerly areas the carp and tench begin to respond to the warming sunlight of spring. They are fished for in summer and autumn but it is a short fishing season, for the frost of late autumn will soon send them into hibernation.

Shoal fish generally remain active throughout the year and so do freshwater predators, the pike, perch and zander. The feeding activities of fish and their life styles have created fishing seasons. These are agreed times at which anglers will deliberately fish for one species or another. Over the years fishing seasons have been imposed by law to ensure that anglers give the fish time in which to breed.

In Europe these legal fishing seasons vary from country to country, but there is an overall pattern in those countries that observe a closed season. Salmon and trout breed in the winter, so they are protected during the cold months of the year. Coarse fish become interested in mating in the spring, so there is a closed season from spring to early summer. Some countries do not ban fishing for coarse fish species at any time of the year.

In recent years, man has begun to stock waters with fish. Often this is done to provide food but also because the rapidly increasing number of people who treat fishing as a sport expect our rivers and natural stillwaters to continue to give the same quantity and quality of fishing. We must, therefore, make use of any water that becomes available, even if we dig holes in the earth to create ponds.

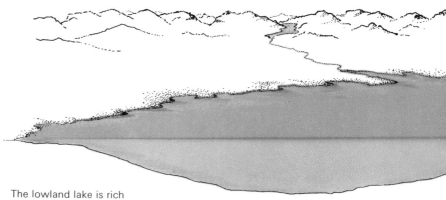

The lowland lake is rich in food and fish. Most freshwater species abound, especially those that tolerate high temperatures and low oxygen levels. Trout will also live in these waters.

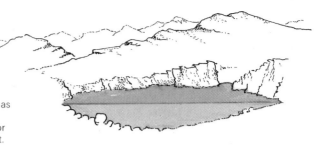

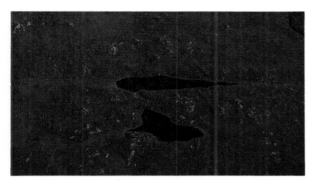

The mountain tarn has water that is always cold. Very little life or vegetation is present. Small trout and char are the only fish found in these tiny highland lakes.

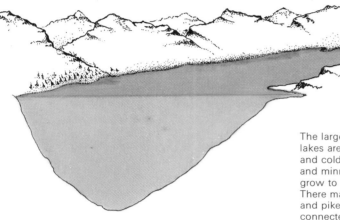

The larger mountain lakes are often very deep and cold. Trout, char and minnows live and grow to small sizes. There may be salmon and pike if the lake is connected to a river system.

As with running waters, our lakes and ponds need oxygen and a whole mixture of animals and plants if they are to support a thriving fish population. The stillwater fishery is more difficult to "read" from the angler's point of view since it is much more liable to changes of water heat than a river. A shallow lake can show a drop in temperature in a few hours. In

The shallow, warm water of the lowland pond or farm pool produces a lush vegetation growth with a possible oxygen deficiency tolerated only by the tench and carp.

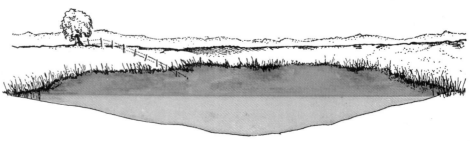

The life cycle of stillwaters

deeper waters we find that a drop in temperature will bring about a mixing of water between the upper and lower water layers. The loss of heat is gradually evened out but the changes will have a marked effect upon the behaviour of the fish and other water creatures.

Some people say that stillwater fisheries are hard to fish in the winter months. What in fact happens is that fish change their way of life. The traditional summer angling species have already migrated down into the deeper areas of the lake where they can pass the cold months buried in the mud. The shoal fish will also tend to move out from the shallow water at the lakeside. This move is both to avoid the cold and to find other sources of food. In winter there is no vegetable growth in the shallows and, therefore, no insect life. Natural food can only be found in the depths, where worm life and the pupa of the summer's insects can be rooted out of the rubbish on the bottom.

Many of our fish are herbivorous, or plant eating, so they have a lean time when the frosts kill off the floating vegetation and the vegetation that grows on the bottom in shallow waters. The predatory fish, who do not change their diet, fare a little better, although pike and perch may have to chase harder to find the small species that make up the food of these freshwater predators. Winter cold and lack of food kill quite a number of the young and very old inhabitants of a lake. The pike will then act as a scavenger, cleaning up all the bodies that fall to the bottom.

With the coming of spring the waters warm, plants begin to throw their new shoots and the larval forms of many creatures will emerge from winter hiding places.

Spring rainfall freshens the water and brings a further supply of oxygen and, as the water plants grow, they too help to improve conditions for the new life within the pond. Never remove plants from the water. Although we like to have clear swims in which to fish, there is a danger, particularly on the small waters, of removing plants that are supporting the life cycles upon which our fishing depends. Free-growing plants that get in the way should be dragged to the side rather than out onto the bank. When rivers are dredged to prevent flooding, it is pretty certain that the fishing will not be the same again for a very long time. In dredging a river, the draglines remove the vegetation and a large amount of the river bed, which is the home of many creatures.

Above: This root from a water plant is covered with invertebrate life, Caddis cases, snails and spawn.

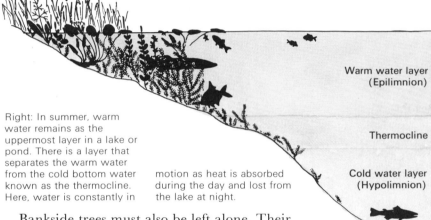

Right: In summer, warm water remains as the uppermost layer in a lake or pond. There is a layer that separates the warm water from the cold bottom water known as the thermocline. Here, water is constantly in motion as heat is absorbed during the day and lost from the lake at night.

Warm water layer (Epilimnion)

Thermocline

Cold water layer (Hypolimnion)

Bankside trees must also be left alone. Their branches may well be in your line of cast, but you need those trees. They provide essential cover, a break in the fish's natural horizon, so that your quarry cannot see your movements at the chosen pitch.

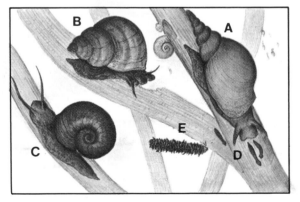

Left: There are a number of different kinds of snails in our rivers and still-waters. The largest, *Limnaea stagnalis* the Great Pond Snail (A), lays many eggs on the underside of water lilies and other surface plants. The Freshwater Winkle *Viviparus viviparus* (B) produces its young alive. The Great Ramshorn (C) looks like a Catherine Wheel. Little flatworms *Planaria* (D) are found under stones and debris. The Caddis larvae (E) builds a home of twigs, stones or snail cases.

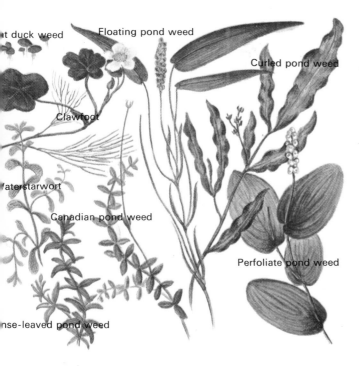

Floating pond weed

t duck weed

Curled pond weed

Clawfoot

aterstarwort

Canadian pond weed

Perfoliate pond weed

nse-leaved pond weed

Above: A spoon that was snagged into the bottom brings up a mass of weed full of freshwater shrimp.

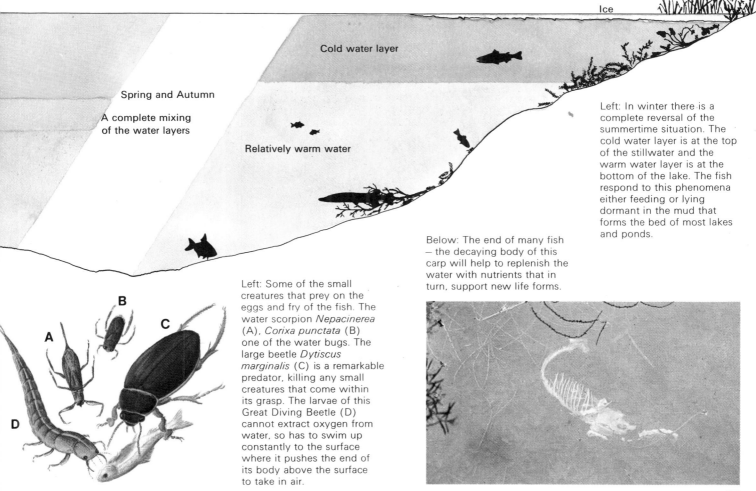

Ice

Cold water layer

Spring and Autumn

A complete mixing of the water layers

Relatively warm water

Left: In winter there is a complete reversal of the summertime situation. The cold water layer is at the top of the stillwater and the warm water layer is at the bottom of the lake. The fish respond to this phenomena either feeding or lying dormant in the mud that forms the bed of most lakes and ponds.

Below: The end of many fish — the decaying body of this carp will help to replenish the water with nutrients that in turn, support new life forms.

Left: Some of the small creatures that prey on the eggs and fry of the fish. The water scorpion *Nepacinerea* (A), *Corixa punctata* (B) one of the water bugs. The large beetle *Dytiscus marginalis* (C) is a remarkable predator, killing any small creatures that come within its grasp. The larvae of this Great Diving Beetle (D) cannot extract oxygen from water, so has to swim up constantly to the surface where it pushes the end of its body above the surface to take in air.

33

The fish of stillwaters

If there is one species that comes to mind as the typical stillwater fish it must be the tench. Ask most coarse fishermen which fish they are opening the new season with and, providing they come from the southerly parts of the British Isles and Europe, they will say the tench. Throughout the cold months of the early spring and into the freshening of the year, tench fishermen everywhere will be planning to pit their wits against this most reliable of fish. The tench fights, pound for pound, far better than most of our coarse fishing specimens. No sophisticated methods or baits are necessary to bring him to the net. A bread bait or a solid, plump earthworm presented on float tackle or lying hard on the bottom as a leger rig will attract him. And what a fine fellow he is.

A good opening method for your tenching effort is to fish a lift-float. It is not the only method and is not necessarily the best throughout the season, but the lift-float style gives a lot of satisfaction. Based on the feeding method of the tench, which is *thought* to be a pronounced head-down attitude, similar to the bronze bream, the rig is fished in such a way that a single swan shot (SSG) is pinched onto the line about $1\frac{1}{2}$ in from the hook. This single shot cocks an antennae float, or something like it, in an upright position. As soon as the tench takes the bait into its mouth it lifts the lead which, in turn, causes the float to lift. There is no better experience than seeing a float lift and then fall flat on the surface of a stillwater in the early dawn of a misty June morning.

Dinner plate or cement sack is what our next fish is often called. The bronze bream is a much maligned fish. He does not fight with the power or stamina of the tench, but sometimes sheer bulk can be the angler's undoing. The bream can grow to huge sizes. Where a water is rich in weed and animals this species grazes, like sheep, in a shoal that moves across the lake bottom with the appetite of a lawnmower.

In certain waters of the East of England and over most of Western Europe there is a smaller relative of the bronze bream. The silver bream, so called, is a smaller fish and can be confused with immature common bream which is of similar colouring. But his sporting fight cannot be compared with the bronze bream.

Fishing a stillwater in early morning and sometimes at dusk, anglers often see a massive disturbance at the water's surface. Although bottom feeders, the mighty common bream often sport themselves by rolling and splashing.

They may well be playing. We do not know exactly what this behaviour means or leads to, but certainly it is a sight to quicken the pulse of any bream angler.

The stillwaters contain another fish that is often seen – and, indeed, fished for – on the surface. The rudd is a magnificent, golden-scaled specimen with brightly coloured fins and deep red eyes. Looking a little like the roach, this fish is found in waters across Europe. It can be fished for in a variety of ways, using conventional float tackle with grub or bread baits or with minute flies on trout fishing gear. One of my favourite summer methods is to fish a slow-sinking maggot under a self-cocking float, occasionally throwing a dozen or so grubs to attract this surface feeder into the swim.

RUDD

Scardinius erythrophthalmus
Below: A similar fish to the roach, having a dorsal fin that begins from behind a line drawn down through the pelvic fins. The rudd has an up-turned jaw and deep red eyes. It may be found in slow-flowing rivers, but is especially associated with stillwaters throughout Europe. Bread, maggots, small insects and bloodworms are the best baits for the rudd.

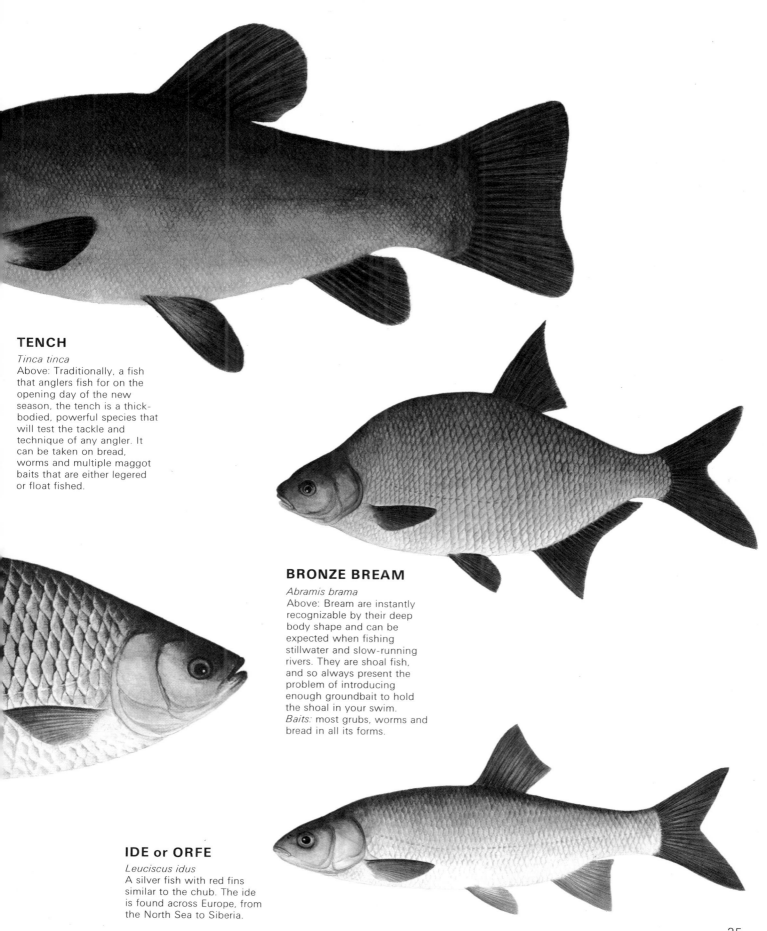

TENCH

Tinca tinca
Above: Traditionally, a fish that anglers fish for on the opening day of the new season, the tench is a thick-bodied, powerful species that will test the tackle and technique of any angler. It can be taken on bread, worms and multiple maggot baits that are either legered or float fished.

BRONZE BREAM

Abramis brama
Above: Bream are instantly recognizable by their deep body shape and can be expected when fishing stillwater and slow-running rivers. They are shoal fish, and so always present the problem of introducing enough groundbait to hold the shoal in your swim.
Baits: most grubs, worms and bread in all its forms.

IDE or ORFE

Leuciscus idus
A silver fish with red fins similar to the chub. The ide is found across Europe, from the North Sea to Siberia.

35

Stillwater populations

Stillwaters can contain the largest and the smallest of our freshwater fish, from the full-bodied carp and massive pike to the minute sticklebacks. Our waters can support a fixed number of healthy fish so long as the conditions are right. If we view the pond as a farm area it can support one or two huge predators with a greater number of smaller juvenile predatory fish, such as perch or pike. The predators will live in association with a vast population of average size shoal fish. Some of these will be fairly large for their type of species. Lastly, there will be a multitude of tiny fish. These will be immature members of the shoal species and predators or adults of the minute species.

The quality of angling in any water can rapidly decline if there are no predators performing their task of regulating the number of fish that live within the water. Without pike or perch a pond will become over-populated with immature fish that will never really reach any size because of the competition for the available food. The result will be a pond full of stunted fish. The problem does not end there. Many of these stunted fish will become breeding fish that spawn, adding to the numbers already competing for the rapidly diminishing food stocks. Nature never intended animals to live in over-crowded conditions. Man, however, has other ideas. He removes predators, believing that they are gobbling up the big fish that he wishes to catch.

There is another reason for a fishery appearing to go into decline. Many enclosed waters lose their fertility, or the ability to provide the amount of natural food demanded by the water creatures that live in it. Farm land needs periodical fertilization if it is to continue to produce plentiful crops. So does water. Modern farming methods brought about a new thinking in terms of scientific management.

When a water environment has suffered, these men seek to refertilize the pond. They do this by cleaning the water, planting new weeds and getting the right balance in the alkaline content or acidity of the water. Then the water can be re-stocked with fish.

In recent years hatcheries have taken to breeding coarse fish. On the continent of Europe where some species, notably carp, are eaten, there are fish farms in most localities. The fisherman benefits from this, since the surplus fish can be used to increase the stock of his fishing water.

Trout, particularly the rainbow variety, have been acclimatized over many years to living in ponds and lakes. Sometimes they are unable to breed naturally. When this happens the mature breeding fish are netted out from the water to be stripped. This means that the eggs from the female and the milt from the male fish are gently squeezed from the abdomen into a bucket. After careful mixing, the eggs are tipped into water-filled trays at the hatchery. A constant supply of clean, fresh water is made to flow continually over the eggs which, with the right temperature (about 40 days at 10°C) can result in a 90% hatching of trout fry. After hatching, the trout are transferred to growing tanks for the most important months of their lives. At 4–5 months the fish are removed from the nursery tanks to be put out into growing ponds where they will be fed high protein pellet diets that ensure a rapid weight gain.

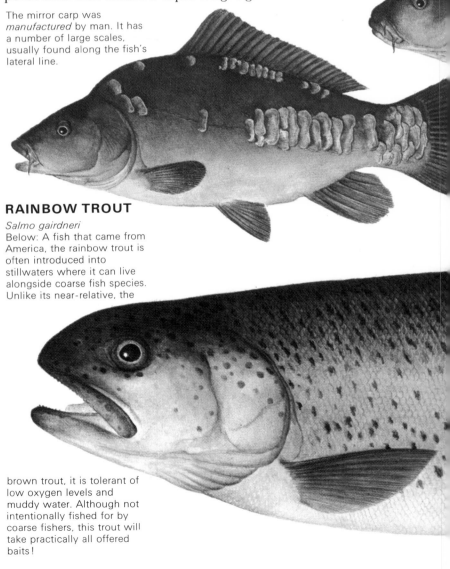

The mirror carp was *manufactured* by man. It has a number of large scales, usually found along the fish's lateral line.

BURBOT

Lota lota
Right: A rare fish in Britain but fairly common on the Continent, the burbot is a member of the cod family that is found in freshwater. It is a bottom-feeder, living in still or slow-flowing waters. Fished for at night or in low-light conditions. The burbot will take worms and grubs and a variety of small deadbaits.

RAINBOW TROUT

Salmo gairdneri
Below: A fish that came from America, the rainbow trout is often introduced into stillwaters where it can live alongside coarse fish species. Unlike its near-relative, the brown trout, it is tolerant of low oxygen levels and muddy water. Although not intentionally fished for by coarse fishers, this trout will take practically all offered baits!

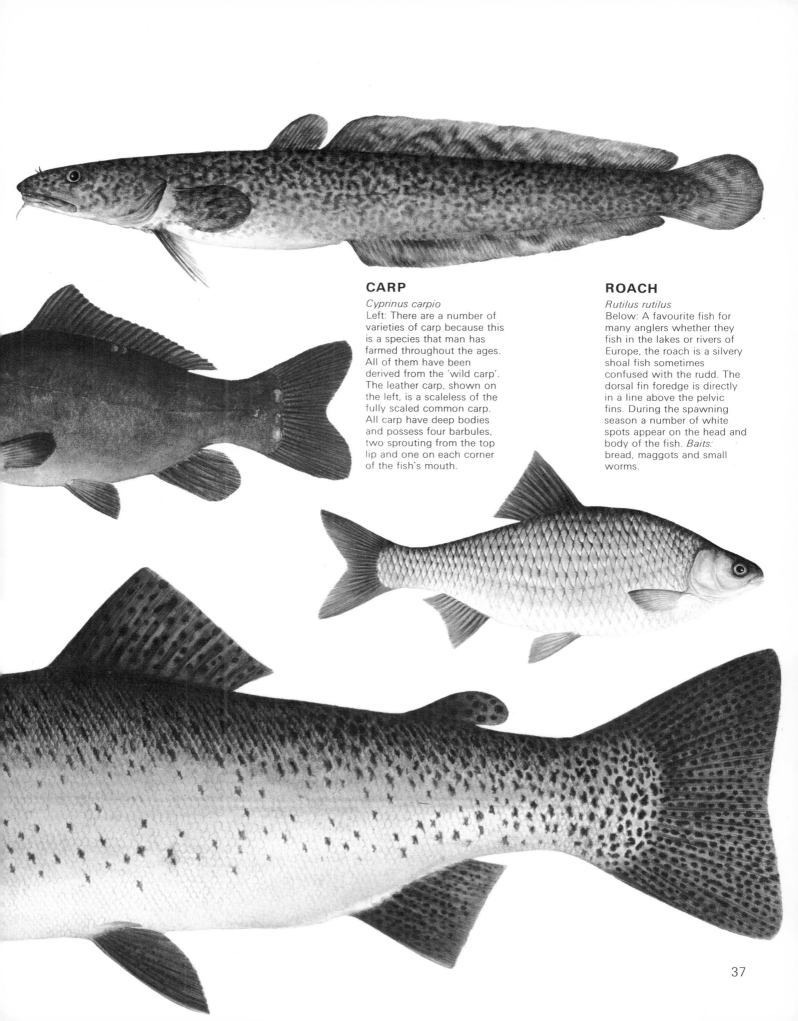

CARP

Cyprinus carpio
Left: There are a number of varieties of carp because this is a species that man has farmed throughout the ages. All of them have been derived from the 'wild carp'. The leather carp, shown on the left, is a scaleless of the fully scaled common carp. All carp have deep bodies and possess four barbules, two sprouting from the top lip and one on each corner of the fish's mouth.

ROACH

Rutilus rutilus
Below: A favourite fish for many anglers whether they fish in the lakes or rivers of Europe, the roach is a silvery shoal fish sometimes confused with the rudd. The dorsal fin foredge is directly in a line above the pelvic fins. During the spawning season a number of white spots appear on the head and body of the fish. *Baits:* bread, maggots and small worms.

Tackle for stillwater fishing

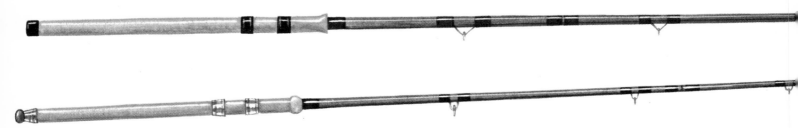

Fishing lakes and ponds can be roughly divided into two separate systems. These are the offering of natural foods, by float fishing or leger methods, or the use of artificial lures to fool the fish into attacking something totally unreal. Of course, we use these two basic systems in running water also but to a lesser extent. If we discount salmon, which records show to be the largest fish ever taken in fresh water, we find that other fish can grow to greater than normal sizes in stillwater situations. There seem to be sound reasons why, for example, a pike can grow larger in a lake rather than in a river. Our pike has the same possibility of catching its food in either environment but it uses up more energy in running water than it would in stillwater. In the river it has to swim against a current which takes up its strength. The energy used up in catching the same amount of food in a lake is obviously much smaller, so the fish grows bigger!

Human beings display similar characteristics. An office worker requires less food than an athlete but if he eats the same amount he will probably grow larger or, at any rate, much fatter.

We would fish for the roach, rudd and perch with fine tackle, almost the same as our river gear. For tench, common bream and carp up

to 10 lb or so, the rod would probably be a leger rod balanced to a line of 6 lb breaking strain. For the larger carp, fish up to 40 lb (for they do grow to that size), we would use a "stepped-up" leger rod with nylon of 14 lb. The same rod is used to leger a deadbait for pike or to handle a large size livebait which many anglers consider the best meal for the really big specimen.

The float rod has its uses for the medium-sized fish and gives great satisfaction to the angler. There is something about watching a float out on the surface. It is a point of focus, demanding great concentration, since it indicates the attentions of fish far below the surface of the stillwater. On the other hand, the leger rig calls for bite indicators that are attached to the rod, either at the tip or at the butt section. These accessories tend to keep our eyes focussed in relative close-up. The float angler, because his indicator is further out, is inclined to see more of what is happening outside the vision area of his own immediate surroundings.

Above: Rods for the leger and float fisherman on still-waters. At the top is a carp rod with low profile rings and threaded Hopton-type tip ring. The test curve of the rod is $1\frac{1}{4}$ lb, allowing the use of lines between $4\frac{1}{2}$ and 6 lb. The lower rod is used by float fishers and is similar in style to that used on rivers and streams. 12 ft long, with high profile rings, it is used with lines of 2 to 4 lb B.S.

Below: The simplest form of leger rigs. An Arlesey bomb is slipped onto the reel line and its movement is stopped with a small split shot. The eyed hook should be tied on with a tucked half-blood knot.

Below: The correct spool loading for the fixed spool reel. Too little line will cause excessive friction over the spool rim shortening your cast. The correctly loaded spool (right) should be filled with nylon to within 1/8 in of the rim.

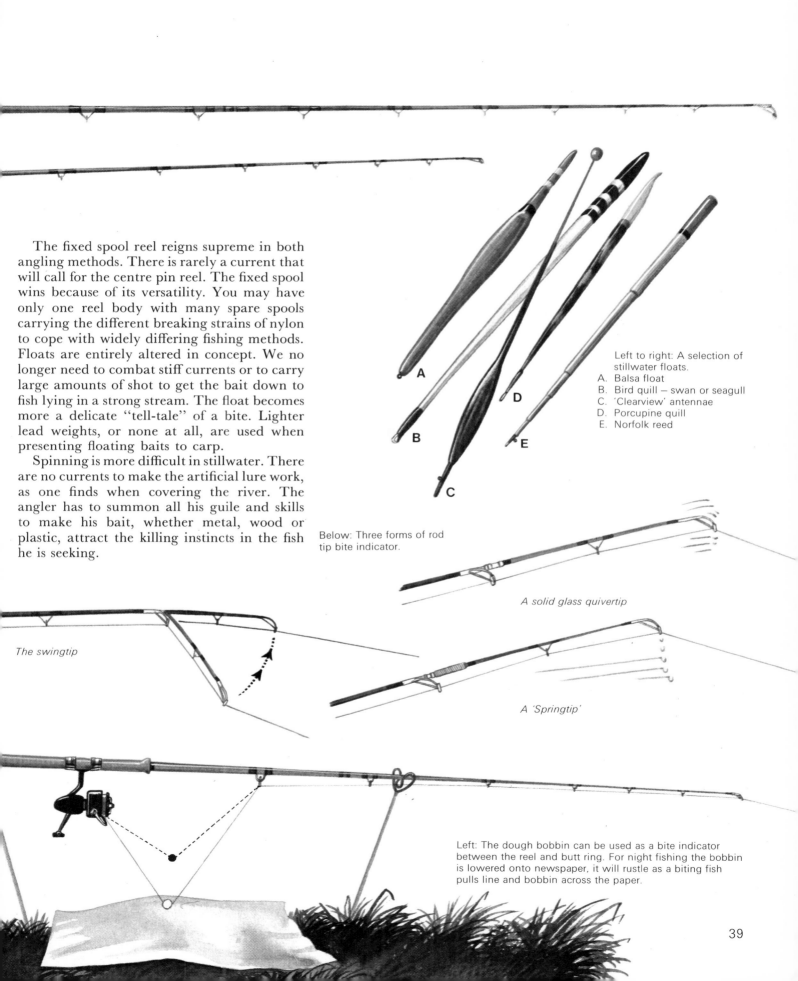

The fixed spool reel reigns supreme in both angling methods. There is rarely a current that will call for the centre pin reel. The fixed spool wins because of its versatility. You may have only one reel body with many spare spools carrying the different breaking strains of nylon to cope with widely differing fishing methods. Floats are entirely altered in concept. We no longer need to combat stiff currents or to carry large amounts of shot to get the bait down to fish lying in a strong stream. The float becomes more a delicate "tell-tale" of a bite. Lighter lead weights, or none at all, are used when presenting floating baits to carp.

Spinning is more difficult in stillwater. There are no currents to make the artificial lure work, as one finds when covering the river. The angler has to summon all his guile and skills to make his bait, whether metal, wood or plastic, attract the killing instincts in the fish he is seeking.

Left to right: A selection of stillwater floats.
A. Balsa float
B. Bird quill — swan or seagull
C. 'Clearview' antennae
D. Porcupine quill
E. Norfolk reed

Below: Three forms of rod tip bite indicator.

A solid glass quivertip

The swingtip

A 'Springtip'

Left: The dough bobbin can be used as a bite indicator between the reel and butt ring. For night fishing the bobbin is lowered onto newspaper, it will rustle as a biting fish pulls line and bobbin across the paper.

Tench fishing methods

Fishing is not just about catching fish. It is a mixture of many things. There is the fun of learning to control fishing tackle and the pride that comes when you know that you can cast just where you wish. There is the never-ending pleasure of watching wild life and of learning about trees, plants and fish. There is the joy of being among beautiful surroundings, sometimes when there is no one else around. Many anglers can enjoy all these things at one time on stillwaters in the early summer.

The fish to try to catch is the tench. You must get to the waterside at first light in mid-June and, if you are lucky, you will find the water still and mirror-like. There will be a thin mist rising from the water and the birds will sing loud and clear. It is almost as if they are trying to tell you in their own way that it will be a long hot day.

The tench is a thick-bodied, powerful fighter that is fond of feeding right down in the mud where it finds the minute worms and insect larvae that make up its diet. When the first frosts of winter cool the water, the tench will disappear down into the mud where it remains dormant until the early spring. Traditionally, the tench is fished on the opening day of the coarse fishing season and it is often called the fish of summer.

This is the time to fish for tench using the *lift method*. Begin by plumbing the depth very carefully indeed. Use line of at least $2\frac{1}{2}$ lb breaking strain. The float is a tiny piece of peacock quill which is fixed to the line at the bottom only. The float is cocked by one shot which should be placed not more than 3 inches from the hook. We call this the lift method because when the tench takes the bait the shot is lifted and the bite is signalled by a lifting of the float.

Although the tench is a shy fish, it may often be attracted into a swim if the bottom is raked smooth by a long-handled garden rake or a heavy drag. It is a good idea to do this raking if you plan to use the lift method because the method works best on a level patch of pool bottom. The raking also adds to the ground baiting by stirring up food for the tench. This food may be water slaters or some of the blood worms (*Chironomus*) which the fish like to eat. These little worms may be used as bait but you will need very fine hooks. The tench is fond of weedy areas, so it is better to use larger hooks and stronger tackle so that you will be able to land the fish.

Below: The overshotted method. As soon as the tench lifts the bait the full weight of shot will pull the float below the surface.

40

Left and far left: Tench can be roused to a feeding frenzy by raking the swim before fishing. This clears the swim of weed allowing the angler's bait to rest in a place that the tench can find. It also produces a cloud of fine silt which clouds the water initially, causing tench to investigate. Minute bloodworms are forced out of the bottom, adding to the value of swim preparation.

Below: Two garden rakes welded together by the tench fisher.

Sometimes the fish will let you know when they have been attracted into the swim. They have a habit of tilting forward to feed and they suck up parts of the pool bed which hold the worms. This sucking releases tiny bubbles of gas which float to the surface. The bubbles often appear in lines which show which way the fish is moving. Bubbles made by the tench are no bigger than pin-heads, while those made in the same way by feeding bream are about as big as peas.

If conditions are not still enough to use the lift method you may take the tench by *over shotting*. Use a larger float, which will ride the ripples on the water. Place enough shot on the line so that the float will just sink if all the shots are off the bottom. Be sure that you have plumbed the depth with care. Place one shot 6 to 9 inches from the hook so that it rests on the bottom. When the tench comes along and picks up your bait the full weight of the shots is placed on the float and the float sinks from view. This tells you that your bait has been taken and it is time to strike and land the fish.

Below: The lift float method. Only one shot is needed to cock the float and tether the bait. When the fish takes the bait into its mouth the weight of the shot is taken off the float, so it falls flat on the water surface.

Legering for tench

There are times, even in summer, when the dawn comes with a chill breeze. If weather conditions have been very hot for a long time the angler may even welcome the wind, because the water temperature may have risen to a point where the fish have become distressed and have stopped feeding. The breeze will lower the temperature and start the fish feeding again. However, the wind does make problems for the angler who may not know how to use a float properly, because the wind will pull the float out of position and it will register false bites. If this happens the answer is to set up legering tackle. One of these is the *link leger*.

The link leger is different from the simple leger because the reel line does not pass through the leger weight. The running line is passed through the eye of a small swivel. A short link of weaker line is then tied to the swivel and the weight is attached at the other end. If the weight becomes snagged then it is the only part of the tackle to be lost.

The link leger is also more sensitive. A fish will signal a bite without being scared by moving the weight. It is best to keep the leger weight as light as possible. Indeed, the weight may be only a single shot if a short distance has to be cast. If you need to cast further, you can add to the weight of the leger by squeezing a ball of very stiff groundbait around it. However, it is a good rule to fish the leger as light as possible. Heavy weights may drag the bait into the mud or into weed growth so that the fish will take a longer time to find it.

When casting leger tackle it is a good idea to cast a little further than the baited area and to wind the tackle back into the swim. This makes sure that the bait falls into the groundbaited area and that the line is nice and straight from the rod tip to the hook. You can then put just enough tension in the line to give you a clear indication when you get a bite. This signal may come as a strong running of the line with

Left: A float-leger rig for tench fishing. Line goes down from the float to a leger weight, which is stopped with a small split shot. (An alternative leger system is shown using a swan shot pinched onto a small swivel.)

all slack being picked up. On hard-fished waters, however, the fish may be suspicious of the bait.

Some anglers are not happy when they have not got a float to watch. Many of these use the *float-leger*. This is a combination of leger and float fishing. The reel line is passed first through the bottom ring of a float and fixed by a couple of turns. It is then taken through a leger weight which is stopped from sliding down to the bait by a small swivel. With this rig, it is better to set the float over depth. You cast out, straighten the line, as in ordinary legering and, after placing the rod on two rod rests, gently turn the reel handle. This tightens the line and the float will cock and can be set at any angle to suit the fisherman. The bite on this rig is usually signalled by a straight running away as the float vanishes. The tench is a very strong fish and it is a mistake to begin fishing without first setting up the landing net. He feeds best in the early morning or evening. Best baits are bread flake, maggots, red worm and lob worms.

Above: A chain of perfect tench lakes, near Tulla, in the County of Clare, Southern Ireland.
Below: Two forms of link leger.
Left: A short length of nylon is folded over the reel line, shots can be pinched onto the nylon link. Should the rig become caught in the bottom, the hook can be released by pulling on the rig which will make the shots pull off the nylon link.
Right: For legering over a known soft, muddy bottom, this rig will prevent the bait sinking down into the mud where a tench could not find it. The nylon link is slipped through a hollow straw or length of polythene, rigid tubing. The link can sink down but the free-running swivel is clear of the cloying mud. Use a small split shot to stop the travel of the lead link.

Float fishing for bream

The tench is not the only fish to send signals which tell the angler that it is around and feeding. The bream will do this, too. Quite often the bream live in the same type of water as the tench and it may be that the fish will move into the area which you had baited for the tench. The bubbles which the rooting bream send up are much larger than those of the tench and the water will colour up quite quickly.

Once this happens it is not too difficult to catch the bream. You can do this by using float fishing tackle. The main thing to remember is that, because of the shape of its body, the bream stands on its head to feed. This means that the line between the hook and the lowest weight should be longer. A short link will mean that the body of the fish will brush against the line and you will get a series of false bites. If you strike at these signals you may frighten the shoal away before you manage to catch a bream. This will not happen if you make the length of line which lies on the bottom about 9 to 12 inches.

When the bream picks up your bait it will also lift the shot which is resting on the bed of the lake. The float will rise and then lie flat. In a moment or two it will begin to settle again and will then be drawn under. That is the moment to strike.

The bream is a big and impressive fish and many anglers like to fish for it as a special hobby. At first they are content to take large numbers of middleweight fish. Perhaps by accident, they then catch one of the large ones. After that their main interest is in seeking out the old grandfather fish. One of the best ways to do this is to concentrate on the area where the first big one was taken, for the bream is a wanderer along set feeding paths.

Right from birth, the shoals roll around, feeding and clearing an area and then moving on like a herd of cattle. As the years go by the shoals get smaller as fish die. Many are killed and eaten by predators. Eventually the big old fish may be one of a very small shoal indeed whose paths cross the feeding trails of other, younger, bream. It is possible to slow down the eternal wanderings of the fish by laying a trail of groundbait into the fishing area and by baiting this pitch heavily.

The fish is fond of cereal-based foods and bread attracts it. You can collect enough groundbait for a session at the bream by saving all the scrap ends of dry bread in the house. Store these in a hessian sack, which will allow

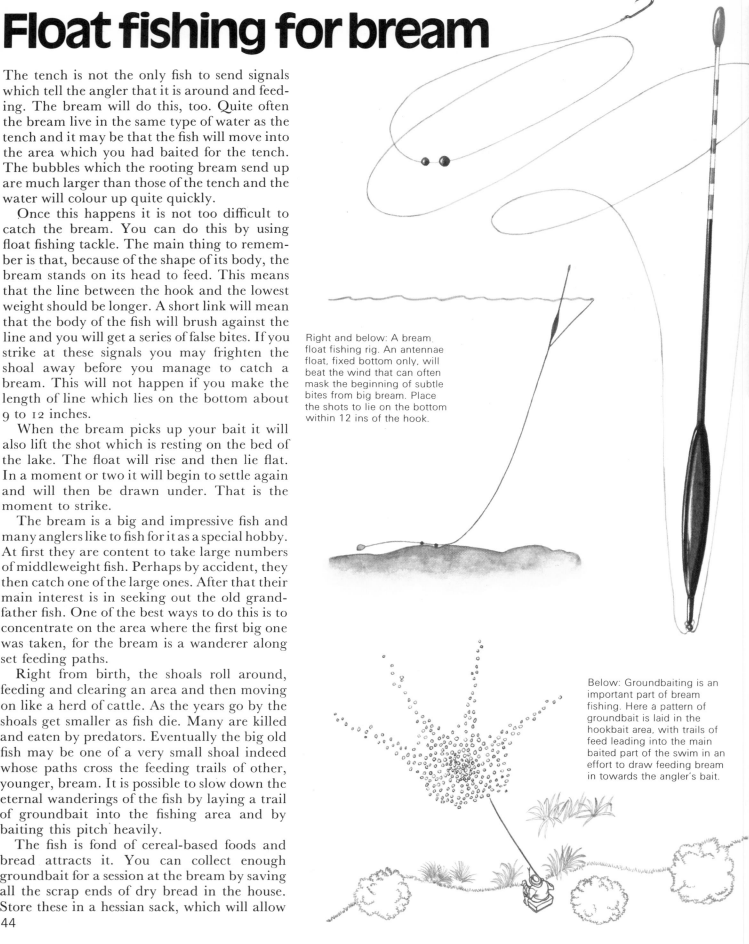

Right and below: A bream float fishing rig. An antennae float, fixed bottom only, will beat the wind that can often mask the beginning of subtle bites from big bream. Place the shots to lie on the bottom within 12 ins of the hook.

Below: Groundbaiting is an important part of bream fishing. Here a pattern of groundbait is laid in the hookbait area, with trails of feed leading into the main baited part of the swim in an effort to draw feeding bream in towards the angler's bait.

Keith Linsell

the air to circulate. Hang the sack in a dry passage which has a good flow of air. These precautions will prevent the bread from becoming sour and mildewed. Mix the bread at the waterside with bran and some of the hookbait which, apart from bread itself, may be worms or maggots. Make sure the mixture is well soaked, because you do not want partly soaked pieces to rise in the water and float away to feed the fishes elsewhere. Big bream have survived because they are shy and sensitive to danger. This is why it is sometimes better to place the groundbait in position before you begin fishing.

No angler will claim that the bream is a very strong fighter but, by virtue of their large flank the bream will test out weak tackle. It is however, an important fish to the angler for, despite its lack of fight, it is plentiful and accommodating. To catch a large specimen requires skill and dedication. What more can anyone ask from a fish?

Above: Big bream are wary fish that sometimes feed best in the hours of darkness. Legering techniques are called for if it is too dark to see a float. Lay a sheet of paper or cloth on the bankside below a bobbin made by folding a piece of paper over the reel line. Illuminate the bobbin with a torch that shines at right angles to the bank — not out over the water! Bites are easily detected because, as the bream takes the bait, the paper bobbin jumps off the paper towards the rod ring.

Right: Big bream place a severe strain on your end tackle. Maintain the breaking strain of the tackle by tying the hook direct to the reel line. When hooked, a bream must be lifted out of the feeding area before it frightens other members of the shoal.

Legering for big bream

During the summer, the bream may feed best in the early evening, throughout the night and at dawn. They do not lose their caution then but it may be the best time to try for a really big fish. Begin by laying the groundbait in the early evening and make proper bankside preparations.

Only have by you what you need immediately. The landing net is the most important thing. Set it up properly and tighten it so that it will not turn and tip the fish back into the water. A groundsheet is also useful. Spread it so that your seat is resting on it. You may need a shaded lamp or torch but direct this so that it does not shine on the water or into your eyes. Use two rod rests so that the handle part of your rod is within easy reach. Keep bait in a sealed container and take care not to allow bits to fall onto the groundsheet in case nocturnal animals are attracted to the area and distract you.

The temperature will fall very quickly once the sun has gone. Make certain that you have plenty of warm clothes with you. It is better to have too many clothes and too much food rather than not enough. You may always remove an extra layer of clothing and take extra food home, but if you once become cold and hungry you will not be able to concentrate on fishing.

The wandering bream may move into the groundbaited area at any time and, while your bait may slow them down, it will not hold them permanently. This is why your preparations must be thorough. Your concentration must not slip. The best way to ensure that your bait is in the proper area is to fish with leger tackle which should be as simple as possible, as you may need to replace it during the night. A simple way to ensure that you always cast into the right place is to practise before night falls. Once you have the correct casting technique under control, mark the reel line to tell you that the bait is in the right place. Tie a stop knot on the line as a mark once the cast has been made. When it gets dark you simply cast out and then wind the line back until you feel the stop knot between your fingers.

The other main problem is how to detect the bite. Perhaps the easiest way to do this is to use a dough bobbin. This is a piece of paste moulded around the reel line just in front of the reel. When a fish bites and the line begins to run, the bobbin moves up towards the first rod ring. There is a danger with this method if the fishing

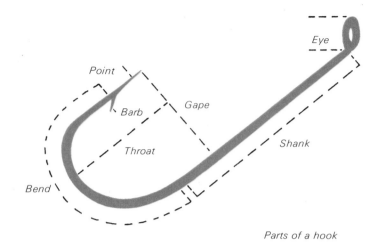

Parts of a hook

is slow. Sometimes the bobbin hardens off and will be pulled up against the rod ring with a jar which may cause the fish to drop the bait before you can strike. Use a piece of silver paper folded over the line as an indicator. It is possible to buy long-lasting "mini" lights which may be used in the same way as the bobbin. Some anglers prefer to use electric bite alarms which make a noise when the line is pulled from between the contacts. Fishing at night can be fun but you should always obey the following rules:

1. Obtain permission before starting to fish. Some stretches of water may only be fished during the day.

2. Always tell your family exactly where you are going and when you expect to return.

3. Take plenty of warm clothes with you even if the day has been extremely warm.

4. Keep your bait in a sealed container.

Right: The long stretch to a bream. Unlike many other species, once the bream's head is up and the fish is beaten. it will come to the net quietly, sliding across the surface of the lake.

46

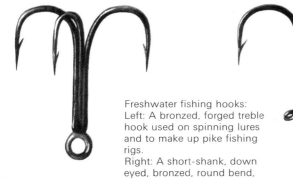

Freshwater fishing hooks:
Left: A bronzed, forged treble hook used on spinning lures and to make up pike fishing rigs.
Right: A short-shank, down eyed, bronzed, round bend, general purpose hook.

Right: A medium shank, straight eyed, forged round bend hook suitable for the larger species, such as carp, tench and bream.

Above left: Fine wire gilt crystal, spade-end hook.
Above right: A beak hook, with turned-up eye.

A B C   **D E F G**

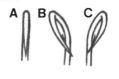

H I J

A. Straight shank.
B. Reversed shank. C. Kirbed shank. D. Knife edge point.
E. Superior point. F. Hollow point. G. Curved-in point.
H. Tapered ring eye. I. Ringed (ball) eye. J. Spade end.

2   4   6   8   10   12   14   16   18   20

Above: Hook chart

Right: The different shanks, points and eyes of hooks.

Float fishing for rudd

Groundbaiting is important when fishing for bream but it is even more important when trying to catch rudd. This golden fish with bright red fins swims in large shoals at the surface of the water. It is fond of weedy areas and the edges of lakes where it browses among the stems of the reeds.

The rudd feeds on insects and snails but will eat pieces of bread which have floated into the reeds. The easiest way for the angler to tempt the fish is to groundbait the outside edge of the reed beds. If there is a breeze this is simple because whole slices of bread will float and lodge against the weed stalks. There they jiggle up and down so that small pieces are broken off and sink slowly towards the bottom. Once the rudd find the bread, it is broken up very quickly as the fish feed directly from it. If there is no breeze the groundbait may be in the form of loose maggots or casters which are fired into the fishing spot by a catapult which has a large cup.

Both bread and maggots fall slowly through the water until the fish snap them up. Your tackle must be rigged to give the same effect. This may best be done by using a float which is self cocking because it has weight built into the lower end. This means that no weight is needed on the line but there is a problem which may make this solution impractical. The rudd is a shy fish and you may not be able to get close enough to the shoal to enable you to use fine, self-cocking floats. You may need to long cast. For this, it is best to use a large float which will carry three or four shots of medium weight. This will give you enough weight to make casting easier. The shot should be bunched less than an inch below the float which should be fixed both top and bottom. You may increase the casting weight by using a piece of bread flake as bait. If you dip this in the water after squeezing it upon the hook it will absorb the water and become much heavier. The rudd will take quite large pieces of flake so a size 12 hook is not too large. It is a good idea to use a combination bait when casting long distances. Use a number 10 hook with two or three maggots and a piece of bread flake squeezed around the top of the shank.

When a shoal of rudd is active and is jostling around the groundbait, the fish do not seem to mind quite large floats and terminal rigs arriving among them. However, they do sense trouble when members of the shoal are hooked. For this reason it is important to play the fish

48

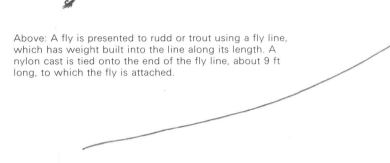

Above: A fly is presented to rudd or trout using a fly line, which has weight built into the line along its length. A nylon cast is tied onto the end of the fly line, about 9 ft long, to which the fly is attached.

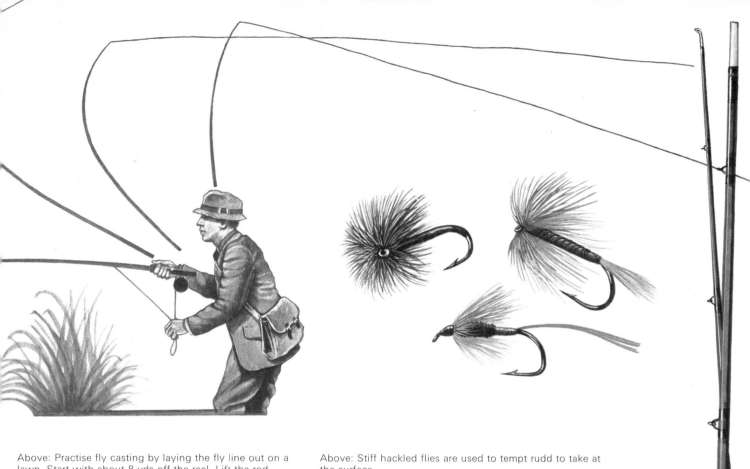

Above: Practise fly casting by laying the fly line out on a lawn. Start with about 8 yds off the reel. Lift the rod sharply, feeling the line travelling back through the air. When you feel it *pulling* on the rod tip, bring the rod forward fairly swiftly. The line should extend with the tip rolling over to lay flat on the grass. After a couple of sessions, go to a stretch of stillwater and practise lifting the line off from the water.

Left: Two rudd fishing styles for stillwater. A. The 'Over-shotted' style depends on a float cocked with one lead midwater and another lying on the bottom. When the fish lifts the bait, the combined weight of both leads will make the float sink below the surface. B. The 'Slow-sinking bait' calls for all the shots to be placed just below the float so that it cocks immediately on casting but the bait is free to sink slowly down through the water. Rudd will frequently take the offering 'on the drop'.

Below: Floats for rudd fishing. A. A balsa stick float. B. A balsa and cane stick.

Above: Stiff hackled flies are used to tempt rudd to take at the surface.

with care. The rudd, as well as the dace and chub, are sometimes caught by anglers using fly fishing tackle. Because there is no weight at the end of the line to aid casting, the technique is different. The fly fishing rod is made to cast a rather heavy line which is tapered down to the hook length rather like a whip. This tackle will deliver a bunch of maggots very well indeed. If you use a floating fly line and grease the nylon leader to within 12 inches of the hook you will see the bite as the line is pulled across the water. Glittering artificial flies like Wickham's Fancy work well, too.

As soon as a rudd has bitten it should be led away from the shoal as quickly as possible as a thrashing fish will soon put the others down. A rudd of any size is not to be despised. A big rudd is a thing of beauty and this, coupled with the fact that the fish comes from such beautiful surroundings, is the reason why, for so many, rudd fishing is such a pleasure.

Right: A typical fly rod and reel.

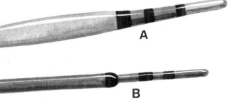

49

Baits for fish

It would be possible to fill several pages with a list of the baits which will take fish. Even a shortened list will certainly include worms, grubs and cereal baits in one form or another. The lobworm is one of the most tempting baits for big fish. This is the large worm which may be found in garden lawns and sports fields on warm and still evenings. Lobworms lie with their tails in the ground and a heavy footfall causes them to stop feeding and to withdraw very quickly indeed. The best way to collect them is to wear soft shoes and to walk very gently. When you spot a worm grasp it firmly at the point where it enters the ground. The bait is deadly for most fish but sometimes just the head or tail fished on its own will be even more effective.

It is not always possible to collect lobworms and many fishing tackle shops sell cartons of a smaller worm known as a brandling. The best place to seek them for yourself is in well rotted compost heaps. You may find in the same kind of place a smaller worm still. This is the red worm. It is a very good bait for taking tench, bream and roach.

Most fish will take a bloodworm. This should not be confused with the earthworm. Bloodworms are, in fact, the larvae of midge flies. They live in the mud at the bottom of most still waters but thrive in those which are slightly polluted. They may be gathered by using a scraper on the end of a stick but they are very small and not an easy bait to use.

Other small baits which will tempt fish and are easy for the angler to obtain include maggots. These are the larvae of flies. The most important is the commercial maggot, which is the larva of the fly known as the bluebottle. It is very common and professional breeders are able to keep fishing tackle shops well supplied with them. They may be used as hook-baits and as loose feed. When they reach the chrysalis stage, they are known as casters. The squatt is a much smaller maggot used mainly as an addition to groundbait. It is bred from the common housefly. Another small maggot is the Pinkie. This one, which is bred from the greenbottle, is also used as a groundbait but is a good hookbait, too.

Some anglers like to breed special maggots as hookbaits. For this, they often breed a large

Above: Life cycle of the angler's bait. There are many kinds of maggots used by fishermen. The most often used is a maggot produced from the eggs of the Bluebottle. After laying the 'blow' on meat, fish or fowl, the eggs develop into a maggot which is used as a hook or loose feed bait. Gradually the grubs skin hardens to become a chrysalis, called a caster, which can also be used to advantage as a bait.

Right: Allen Edwards preparing his groundbait for a bream fishing session. The cereal content is crumb and pigmeal into which a handful of lobworms are added to draw the bream into a feeding mood.

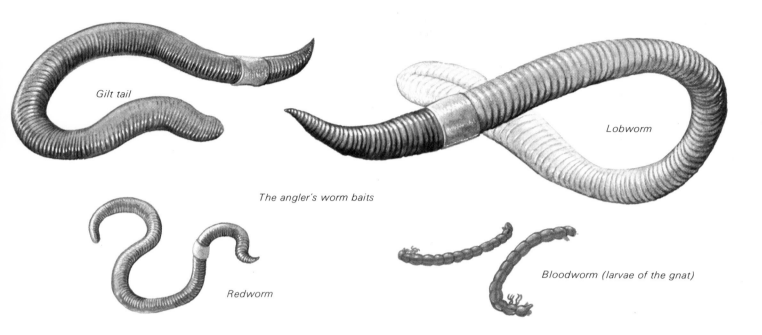

Gilt tail

The angler's worm baits

Lobworm

Redworm

Bloodworm (larvae of the gnat)

and succulent maggot known as a gozzer. This is bred from a fly which is a close relative of the bluebottle. Amateur breeders set about raising these maggots by using fresh dead meat which may be a pigeon or game bird. The fly is different from the others because it prefers to lay its eggs in the dark. Place the meat in a large biscuit tin. If a small hole is made in the lid, only the correct fly will enter and lay eggs. All of the maggots make good baits but extra care should be taken to dispose of them at the end of every fishing session.

Cereal baits include seed baits like wheat, hemp and tares. These should be brought to the boil and simmered until they split. Like most baits they work best when fresh.

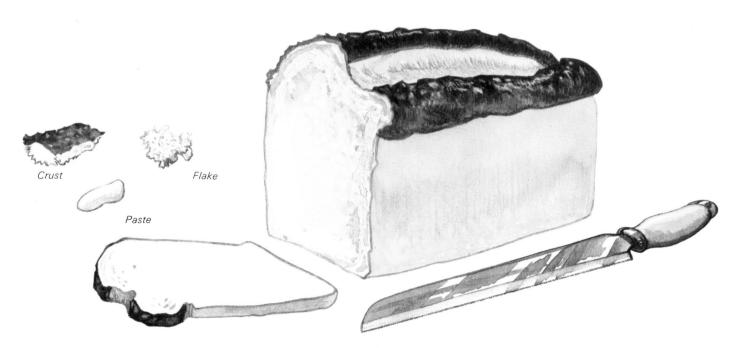

Crust

Flake

Paste

Fishing for carp

Next to the salmon and the pike the fully grown carp is the biggest of all our freshwater fish and catching a big specimen is always exciting sport. Although there is only one species of true carp, *Cyprinus carpio*, (to give it its proper name) the three varieties found in our waters can all be caught by the same methods.

Fishing with a floating crust: This is a delicate searching form of fishing in which a crust, without any weights attached, is cast into the path of the cruising fish. The crust acts as a surface bait and the idea is to attract the carp as they patrol the edges of the water or pool or nose into floating weedbeds.

Preparing your bread bait is simple but there are a few points to watch. First of all, tear off a piece of crust from the side of a new loaf. Push the point of your hook down through the crusty side of the bread. And now you must be careful. When the point and bend of the hook come through the crust, give them a twist before you pull the hook back into the crust.

The bread will now be firmly on the hook. You must dip it into the water to give it enough weight for you to cast it properly. When you have soaked the bread – just a few seconds in the water is sufficient – you must swing the baited hook out onto the water in a gentle movement. The crust should land on the water with the shank of the hook uppermost.

This is so that a feeding fish can nudge the bait with its mouth without feeling the shank of the hook and the attached nylon line. A taking fish will tend to suck the bait in with a "slurping" sound – a hungry carp has no manners! Once the fish has taken the bait be sure to give him time to turn and begin to move off before you make any attempt to strike.

If you know that big carp are present in the water, leave the bale arm open on your reel and pre-set the slipping drag to about half the breaking strain of the line. Then, when your fish makes its run with the bait, close the bale arm, allow the line to tighten. Then strike firmly. Any further breaking effect can be made by pressing your index finger onto the rim of the exposed reel spool or by gradually tightening up the clutch as the fish begins to slow down – but always be on the alert for a sudden dive or a sharp change of direction.

Float fishing: This is another successful method of catching carp but there is one important point to watch. Carp are extremely sensitive to any unnatural drag on the bait, so the float must be kept as light as possible – just sufficient

Above: Allen Edwards extends his landing net to a mirror carp. His finger presses gently on the rim of the spool to control possible last minute dashes by the hooked fish.

Great care should be taken in removing the hook from a carp. The skin is tough so grasp the hook shank firmly to make a positive removal operation.

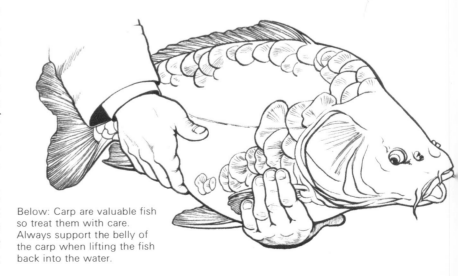

Below: Carp are valuable fish so treat them with care. Always support the belly of the carp when lifting the fish back into the water.

Below: Four types of carp hook. All four hooks are strong with needle-sharp points and small barbs.

| The Model Perfect | A Richard Walker | A Stiletto | The VMC Specimen |

to carry the bait and shots. My own favourite is an antennae float with a balsa wood body. When carrying the bait and leads, this leaves just the slim antennae stick above the water surface. I find this gives me the smallest possible drag and the greatest sensitivity.

Legering: Fishing the leger over soft muddy bottoms or weeded bottoms is another technique but this is usually only done in deep water and it can present one tricky problem. If you use a leger weight fixed in the normal and traditional way, the bait tends to be pulled down into the mud or weed where the carp cannot find it. There are two ways of avoiding this. One way is to present the bait in a semi-floating manner. This is called a "balanced crust" bait and all you have to do is to press the crust bait firmly onto a piece of flattened bread paste. The bait is still fine food for the hungry fish but it will not be heavy enough to

Below: A. Floating crust bait for carp cruising below the water's surface.
B. When fishing over thick weed it is a good idea to balance the crust ensuring that it fishes in mid-water. Do this by pressing a piece of paste firmly onto the crust.
C. Bait presented on a link-leger system will leave the bait clear of mud and weeds, although the lead may sink into the soft bottom.

Carp can be taken on float tackle. Use an antennae float with the bulk shot below the float. One fairly large shot will tether the bait. Bites are indicated by a lift or by the float sliding away purposefully.

Crucian carp, roach and perch

sink into the mud. The addition of the bread paste to the bait helps make a good cast.

Another and very simple way of avoiding the mud and the weeds at the bottom is to use a link leger. In this system the lead is attached to a three-way swivel by a yard or so of nylon. The lead can sink into the weed or mud but the bait will sit on the soft bottom and the fish will be able to find it. Moreover, the fish will feel hardly any drag since the line does not pass through the leger weight.

Whichever system you decide to use when you fish for carp you must be prepared for thrills. A big carp has tremendous strength and great endurance. He won't give in easily. There are some obvious hazards to avoid. Try not to let your fish fight his way into heavily weeded areas of the water or dive beneath a sunken tree. Never let him have a slack line. And – another useful tip – when you go fishing for carp take the biggest landing net you can get and keep your fish in a large knotless keepnet.

Big carp provide excitement but there is a small carp which will provide entertainment. It is called the Crucian Carp (*Carassius carassius*). This beautiful little fish is often found in very small ponds and will survive in conditions which other members of the carp family will not stand. There can sometimes be swarms of the fish and catching them can be great fun. It is important to remember that the fish live in water which usually has a very fine, silty bed. This means that it is not a good thing to have weights very close to the bait. Careful plumbing of the depth is a good idea and the bait should tumble slowly through the water so that it rests very gently on, or a fraction above, the bottom. Careful groundbaiting is a help when fishing for crucians. Make up a mixture which includes biscuit crumbs or a very small addition of sugar.

The crucian is a very dainty feeder and if your tackle is too coarse or not properly rigged you will get many bites which you will not see. The same may be said of small and stillwater roach. Your tackle should be delicate and your casting should be careful. The main aim is to allow the bait to tumble very slowly through the water and not to bury it in the silt.

The groundbait for roach will, however, be different. This is because the roach will feed at all depths. If you mix finely ground bread so that it creates a cloud effect in the water, the fish will take your tumbling bait. Best baits for both crucians and stillwater roach include

Right: Perch paternoster rig. The perch is a predator. It will take the small fry of other species as well as worms and grub baits. To catch a big specimen the paternostered livebait is regarded as one of the best methods. Instead of using a three-way swivel to join the hook link and lead, take the reel line through the top eye of swivel with a split shot acting as a stop to the length of the link. This method allows a crafty perch to take the offering without feeling too much resistance on the tackle. Obviously, a tight line must be kept to the lead so that you can feel the take and react by gently lowering the rod top until the take develops into a positive run.

Below: These young lads live alongside a canal, in Ireland, where fine perch can be taken regularly. Their favourite bait is a lobworm or brandling from the farm manure heap.

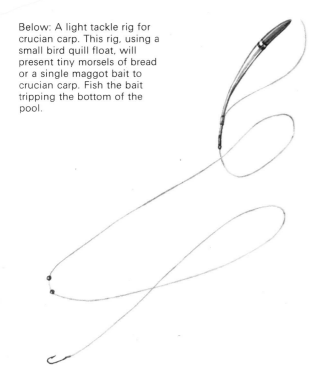

Below: A light tackle rig for crucian carp. This rig, using a small bird quill float, will present tiny morsels of bread or a single maggot bait to crucian carp. Fish the bait tripping the bottom of the pool.

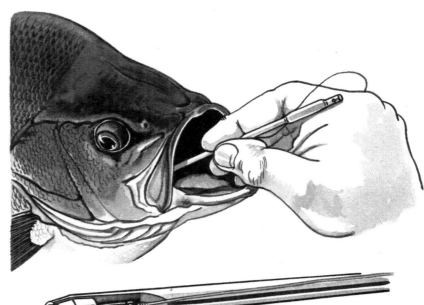

Above: The slotted disgorger. It will not harm the fish when used properly and with care. Slide the open slot over the nylon, keeping the line fairly tight. Run the jaw of the disgorger down over the eye and shank of the hook. A gentle push down to free the barb and the hook can be removed easily.

maggots, casters, breadflake, small redworm and sweetcorn. You can buy sweetcorn in tins from the grocer. There are two things to watch when using it. Firstly, transfer the bait at home, from the tin into a linen bag. This is because you may cut yourself on the edge of the tin or by mistake leave it lying around, where it will cut sheep or cattle. The second thing is not to eat the bait yourself! It is delicious. You fish the bait by putting one or two kernels upon

Below: Crucian carp thrive in the tiniest of pools. They like weedbeds where the fish root for the small water creatures that breed within the lush vegetation.

a size 12 hook. It will also account for the larger carp, and tench are fond of it too.

Some stillwaters tend to produce large populations of small fish. These may be made up of a mixture of crucians and roach and will almost certainly include the perch (*Perca fluviatilis*). This very handsome fish is present in most waters and it may be in close company with the ruffe or pope (*Gymnocephalus cernua*). Both of these fish may be taken on small redworm or maggot. You may use the same basic tackle as for the other stillwater species but use a larger hook. A size 12 is about right. It is not so important to present the bait at the correct depth and if the worm finally falls and fishes a few centimetres above the bottom it will work very well.

The bite indication from a perch is quite distinctive. The float will bob, bob and bob again before sliding under. This is because the fish swims up to the bait and sucks it in and then blows it out again. It may do this two or three times before deciding that the bait is good enough to eat. Perch may grow quite large because they will feed on small fish. You can catch them by fishing at the same depth with a minnow which is hooked through the top lip only.

Spinning for perch and pike

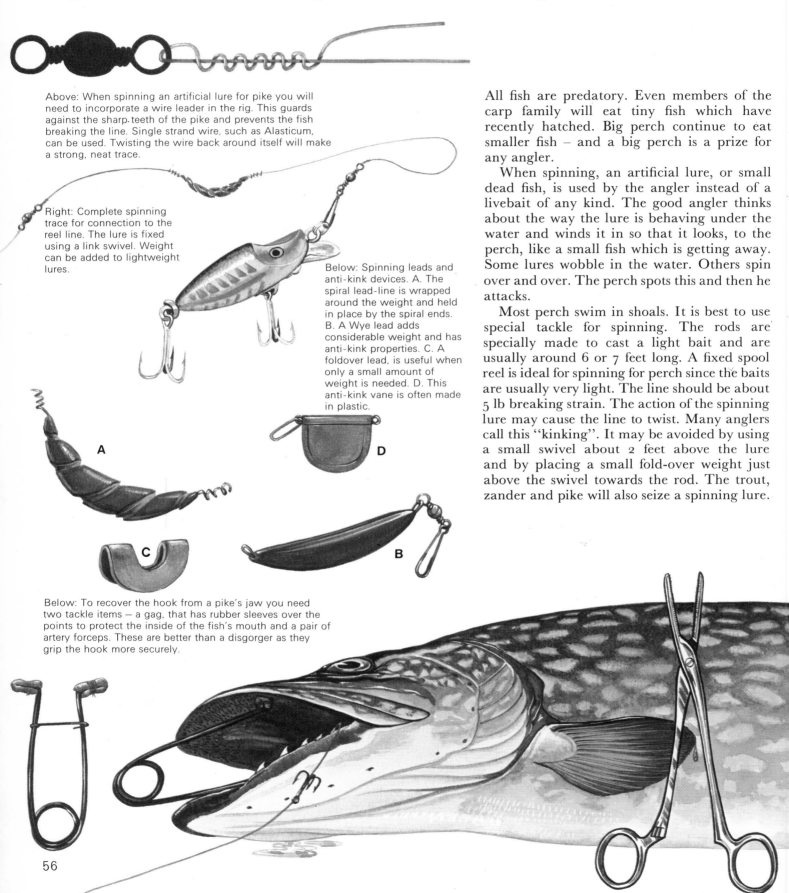

Above: When spinning an artificial lure for pike you will need to incorporate a wire leader in the rig. This guards against the sharp teeth of the pike and prevents the fish breaking the line. Single strand wire, such as Alasticum, can be used. Twisting the wire back around itself will make a strong, neat trace.

Right: Complete spinning trace for connection to the reel line. The lure is fixed using a link swivel. Weight can be added to lightweight lures.

Below: Spinning leads and anti-kink devices. A. The spiral lead-line is wrapped around the weight and held in place by the spiral ends. B. A Wye lead adds considerable weight and has anti-kink properties. C. A foldover lead, is useful when only a small amount of weight is needed. D. This anti-kink vane is often made in plastic.

Below: To recover the hook from a pike's jaw you need two tackle items — a gag, that has rubber sleeves over the points to protect the inside of the fish's mouth and a pair of artery forceps. These are better than a disgorger as they grip the hook more securely.

All fish are predatory. Even members of the carp family will eat tiny fish which have recently hatched. Big perch continue to eat smaller fish – and a big perch is a prize for any angler.

When spinning, an artificial lure, or small dead fish, is used by the angler instead of a livebait of any kind. The good angler thinks about the way the lure is behaving under the water and winds it in so that it looks, to the perch, like a small fish which is getting away. Some lures wobble in the water. Others spin over and over. The perch spots this and then he attacks.

Most perch swim in shoals. It is best to use special tackle for spinning. The rods are specially made to cast a light bait and are usually around 6 or 7 feet long. A fixed spool reel is ideal for spinning for perch since the baits are usually very light. The line should be about 5 lb breaking strain. The action of the spinning lure may cause the line to twist. Many anglers call this "kinking". It may be avoided by using a small swivel about 2 feet above the lure and by placing a small fold-over weight just above the swivel towards the rod. The trout, zander and pike will also seize a spinning lure.

The pike prefers to take his food from ambush. His teeth may cut the line, so anglers who fish for the pike will use a wire trace between the swivel and the lure. A simple way to make one of these is to use a coil of Alasticum wire but only use this trace once because they kink and lose their strength.

The pike is accustomed from an early age to scooping up the residue of its own depridations, and the modern fisherman turns this to his own advantage by using baits that are long dead. Herring and sprats are ideal for this. They are readily available, are relatively inexpensive and can be kept frozen for long periods of time. But there comes a time when the pike angler has to admit that while the small pike may well fall

victim to his lures the crafty old female pike, with her surfeit of cunning, stays stoney-eyed and immune. In such circumstances the pleasure angler will introduce the ultimate in methods and, if he is to take the fish, is compelled to revert to the very effective livebaiting tactics.

Right: Some anglers prefer to use a gaff when pike fishing. If you use one, use it properly! Never gaff the pike in the body. Always play the fish out, bringing it gradually towards you. Then lifting its head, insert the gaff in the tissue behind the jaw bone. Beach the pike and you will find that the gaff has done little damage to it.

Below: Most anglers prefer to net a big pike — after all there aren't many of the really large specimens around! It is a two man job. Draw the fish over a waiting net that has been lowered well in advance of the fish coming close-in. Keep the clutch loose, with finger pressure providing most of the drag on the reel for when the pike sees the net it may well decide to have a last dash for freedom.

Pike fishing

When spinning for pike the gear should be stronger throughout. Eight to ten lb. breaking strain line is satisfactory. The hooks on the lures should be larger and it is important to sharpen these every time they are used. A small carborundum stone will do this very well. The mouth of the pike is very bony and has ridges of sharp teeth which slope towards the throat. This makes the hooking of the fish a problem unless the tackle is strong and the hooks sharp enough.

The pike is really a lazy fish. It prefers to lie and wait for food to swim into range. It will not chase food over long distances as will the trout and perch. Big old pike will often act as scavengers and pick up dead fish from the bottom. Wise anglers know this and catch the pike by legering with small herrings or sprats as bait. The dead fish should be rigged so that there are two sets of trebles. One is fixed in the tail of the bait and the other towards the head. The tail of the bait is nearest the top of the rod. A pike which scoops up dead baits is quite likely to hold it for a few seconds only before turning it head first and sliding towards the stomach. For this reason it is a good idea to place a float on the line. Any movement of the float means that master pike has grabbed the bait and a long, steady, strike should be made. If the pike is given too long to swallow the bait it will mean that the pike cannot be released unharmed.

Many anglers are afraid of the pike. This is a pity and the pike should be treated with as much care as any other fish. One of the ways to do this is to use a special gag as an aid in removing the hooks. This gag may be bought from tackle shops and is really a spring which stops the pike from closing his jaws on the angler as he unhooks the fish (see previous page). The shop-bought gags may be improved by fixing small circles of cork on the sharp prongs of the gag or by binding them with adhesive tape.

When the jaws of the pike are held open the hooks should be removed with care. Long handled artery forceps are ideal for this operation.

It is possible to take the pike by using deadbaits which are worked by the angler to look like a wounded fish which is trying to get away. The rod and line are the same as when spinning but the small fish is fixed on with the head pointing up the line towards the rod tip. A single carp hook is whipped onto a trace and this is passed through both lips of the bait. A

Above: The paternostered live bait rig for pike. This is a useful rig for fishing known pike holes, whether in a river or lake. The bait can be dropped into the pike lair and kept stationary. Fish the live bait about 12 to 18 ins above the bed of the river, so it is clear of thick bottom-growing weeds. Use a flexible wire trace between the three-way swivel and the single hook.

Below: Allen Edwards with a fine pike of 14 lbs.

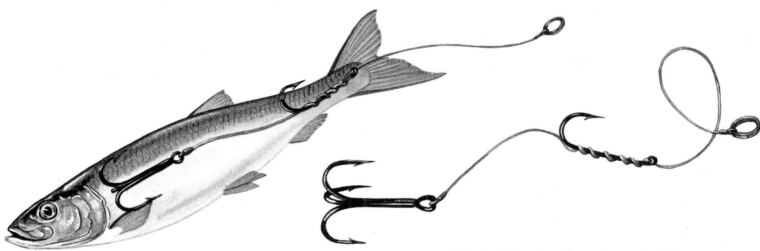

Below: A 'Sink and Draw' rig for pike fishing. This rig offers a fishing method as an alternative to spinning an artificial lure. It is similar to the deadbait tackle, except it has a barrel lead which is inserted into the mouth of the bait to give weight to cast and to make the bait sink easily. The fishing method is simple but effective. Cast the bait out, let it sink, then draw the rod tip up to make the bait rise in the water. Lower the rod tip whilst winding in a small amount of line. In the meantime the bait will flutter back to the bottom. Repeat the action until the bait is drawn back to your feet or it is grabbed by a waiting pike. Always fish twice over the same ground. The first 'sink and draw' can wake up the pike, arousing his hunting instincts; a second bait travelling through the swim will force it to take action!

Above: The legered deadbait rig for pike. Using a herring for bait is probably best as it is an oily fish and gives off a strong scent to marauding pike. Form a rig from flexible or single-strand wire. Fix the treble into the herring behind the gill-case. Adjust the position of the single hook to the size of your bait, then insert it securely into the wrist of the tail (the tough muscle area just ahead of the tail). Finish off the rig with a strong split ring or swivel.

treble hook is placed on the end of the trace and one prong is hooked into the bait near the tail. The fish should be cast out and worked back with plenty of movement.

Although it is a method which appears to be losing favour some anglers prefer to catch pike by livebaiting with a gudgeon, small roach or rudd. When this is done it is best to place a fairly big float on the line so that the little fish will swim about 2 feet above the bottom. A small bullet should be slipped onto the line so that it is stopped at the swivel. A short trace and a single number 2 carp hook completes the rig. If the bait is hooked through the top lip only it may be released if not taken by a pike.

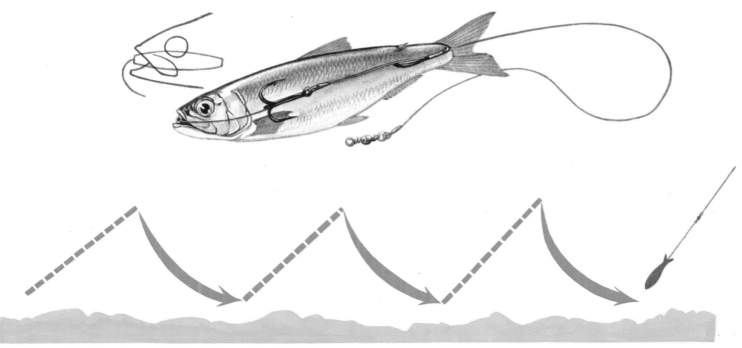

Saltwater fishing

The water area of the earth's surface is twice as great as the land area. About 92 per cent of this water is salt to the taste. Only a relatively small amount is freshwater. All the rivers, lakes and inland seas of the world add up to very little when measured against the oceans.

Not all of the salt-water areas are of interest to sea anglers, since many are either too deep or too far offshore for the average sportsman. We need to find our fishing in the narrow band of shallow water that surrounds most of the land masses. We shall find the angler, with his rod and line up to 20 miles out from the seashore where the depth approaches 50 fathoms.

The shore fisherman, for whom this introduction to saltwater fishing is intended, is concerned with the first 200 yards out from the tideline. He is limited by the distance he can cast and by the movement in or out of the tidal waters from the shore. This inter-tidal zone, happily for the shore fisher, is among the richest food producing sea areas. The fish we seek to catch know that the inshore waters contain these animals and algae, so they swim in to search the ground for them and to feed upon them.

There are seasons for breeding and for growth in the sea just as there are in our freshwaters. As the seasons change so the fish adapt themselves to a different diet. In the spring they may well feed on the eggs and young of many inshore-breeding species. Summer will find them chasing the young of all the fish that spend their early years in the shallow water. As autumn comes the fish may have to alter their feeding to picking off shellfish from the rocks and shellbeds, since the fish fry will have grown stronger and wiser, enabling them to escape more easily. With the coming of winter some fish will migrate to deeper water to escape from the cold. Others will grub around in the debris on the sea bed to find worms in the mud and sand. When winter storms drive the small fish into shallow waters the bigger and stronger species will follow them in, knowing that small fish have a hard time trying to swim against the battering of wind and wave.

The shore fisherman must learn something of the environment in which he sets out to get his sport and, possibly, a meal for his family. A close study of the inshore areas, preferably during the lowest tides when a fisherman can see most of what is usually below the waves, must add to the knowledge so necessary to the making of a good sea angler.

Above: Tide strength varies throughout the 12½ hour phase. The strongest ebb and flow will be felt in 3rd–4th and 9th–10th hours.

Northward movement of warm water species during summer, e.g. Black Bream.

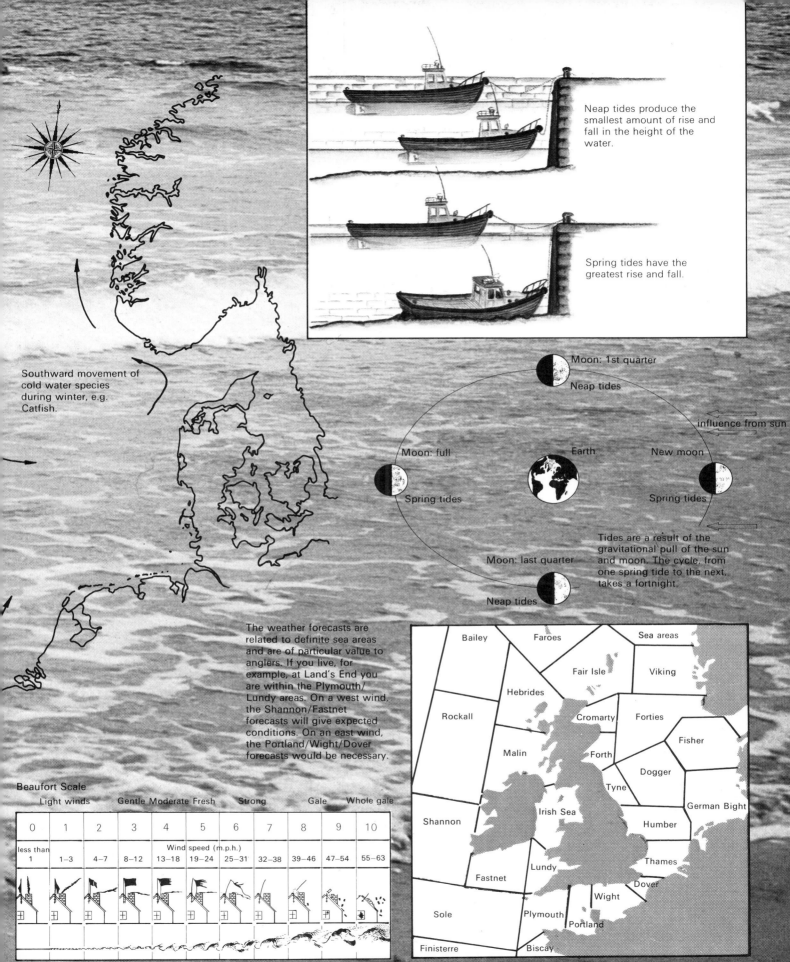

Neap tides produce the smallest amount of rise and fall in the height of the water.

Spring tides have the greatest rise and fall.

Southward movement of cold water species during winter, e.g. Catfish.

Moon: 1st quarter
Neap tides

influence from sun

Moon: full
Spring tides

Earth

New moon
Spring tides

Moon: last quarter
Neap tides

Tides are a result of the gravitational pull of the sun and moon. The cycle, from one spring tide to the next, takes a fortnight.

The weather forecasts are related to definite sea areas and are of particular value to anglers. If you live, for example, at Land's End you are within the Plymouth/Lundy areas. On a west wind, the Shannon/Fastnet forecasts will give expected conditions. On an east wind, the Portland/Wight/Dover forecasts would be necessary.

Beaufort Scale

Light winds			Gentle	Moderate	Fresh		Strong		Gale		Whole gale
0	1	2	3	4	5	6	7	8	9	10
less than 1	1–3	4–7	8–12	13–18	19–24	25–31	32–38	39–46	47–54	55–63

Wind speed (m.p.h.)

Sea areas

Bailey · Faroes · Fair Isle · Viking · Hebrides · Rockall · Cromarty · Forties · Malin · Forth · Fisher · Dogger · Tyne · German Bight · Shannon · Irish Sea · Humber · Lundy · Thames · Fastnet · Dover · Wight · Sole · Plymouth · Portland · Finisterre · Biscay

The four shorefishing habitats

Although saltwater ebbs and flows onto every part of our coastline it does not always produce fishlife; neither is it always the same in character. Fish come into the shallow, inshore, waters to breed, live and seek their food. The shingle beach is generally steep in appearance. This sharp slope continues for some distance under the water where it may then slope less or even-out onto a flat bottom. Shingle beaches are associated with vigorous current and tidal action. It is the strength of tides that throws up the shingle to form the beach.

Because of the strong currents very little vegetation will grow in the water. The plants cannot get a good grip on the shingle or into the sand that forms the sea bed. The main source of food for fish would be those animals that can burrow into the bottom, hiding from the power of the sea to emerge at periods of slack water. Worms are best adapted to this life, and there are also cockles and other shellfish that burrow. Often, these shingle beaches fish best when there is a strong surge onto the bottom that drives these creatures out to the searching fish.

Sandy beaches are gentle in sloping down to the water with slow current flows and weaker tidal action. The easier water movement allows many more creatures to live off the sandy beach. However, if the beach faces west you will find that it is often pounded by long, creaming breakers that are the product of the ocean swells built up by winds many thousands of miles out in the Atlantic. This type of sandy beach appears to be barren of food life. Sometimes they can be, but more often they have some worm life and colonies of tiny fish, called sandeels, that live down in the sand. The breakers, when they turn and smash onto the sand, force the worms and fish out to be taken by fish that know they are there.

Basically, there are two types of rocky shore; the cliffs that fall directly down into deep water with perhaps just a few ledges on which an angler can scramble. Then there is the sandy beach with fingers of rock running out into the sea. The water will be shallow, but the food opportunities are improved as there is another source of food for the fish growing on the spurs of rock.

With the first category of habitat, fish will have a permanent home. There is plenty of depth ensuring water at all stages of the tide with a plentiful supply of food. The seas may, at times, crash onto the cliffs but most of the

Above: A typical rock fishing situation, Spanish Point on the coast of Clare.

Above: The rocky shore has the most prolific growth of weeds with a varied invertebrate animal life. In bad weather the fish will be able to find some cover among the rocks and gullies that make up this type of sea angling habitat. Shell fish baits can easily be found.

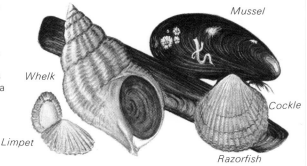

Mussel

Whelk

Cockle

Limpet

Razorfish

Above: These are the most useful shellfish for the angler's bait box. The limpet lives on the rock faces, and fixes itself so tightly it has to be prised off with a metal tool. Mussels grow in colonies on rocks, wooden piles and harbour walls. The cockle and razorfish are burrowing animals whilst the whelk seeks deep water habitats.

disturbance to the water will be confined to the upper layers. There will be plenty of rocks and crevices into which the local fish population can creep in times of stormy weather. Life on the mixed rock-sandy beach habitat will not be quite so easy. Fish will have to move in and out of the feeding area as the tides come and go, exposing a good part of the rock to the air and sunlight. Fish species found off the rock fingers will be those that come in to feed rather than those that intend living there.

Above: A shorefishing competition on a shingle beach on the coast of North Wales.

Above: A gently-sloping sandy beach in the West of Ireland.

Above: The single beach has a fairly steep gradient. The shingle and larger stones, that form the beach, are constantly moving with the strong tidal action. This means that the beach is not capable of supporting many of the soft-bodied creatures nor can shellfish live in it.

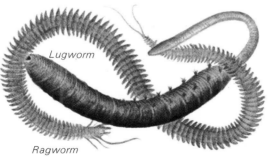

Lugworm

Ragworm

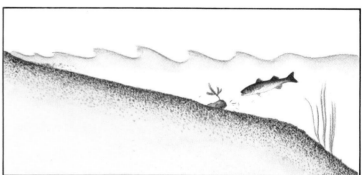

Above: The sandy beach has a gentle slope that allows most worms to live in the sand. Cockles and other burrowing shellfish may be found, together with the sandeel, in the damp sand near to the waterline. Some weed may be able to grow, particularly where there is shelter from strong currents.

An estuary is the opening where a river flows into the sea. Because there is an overlap of fresh and saltwater, fish species that choose this ground will be those that are tolerant of the freshwater content. Water current flows can be fierce as the tide ebbs and flows but with a wide estuary there are times when the flow is gentle enough to bring fish in. The river flow will bring down mud and silt. These make highly fertilized mudflats and banks, rich in marine creatures. But you will find weed growth if

Above: Both of these marine worms make superb angling baits. The lugworm lives in mud and sand mixtures where it forms a U-shaped burrow. The ragworm tends to live in more muddy habitats like harbour mouths. Both species are colonial invertebrates, with many thousands of worms in a confined area.

there are rocky outcrops that hide crabs and form holdfasts for molluscs and seaweeds.

Lastly, there are the man-made fishing situations, such as harbours, piers and jetties that form a natural disturbance to the flow of tide. All kinds of life will dwell on these structures. If they are near to human habitation the fish will come to know that man throws his waste into the water. Much of what we regard as rubbish is, in fact, food for fish and other animals on land as well.

63

Fishing from the shingle beach

When man first took a bait to the seashore to catch food, he probably hurled the hookbait out tied to a stone with the line lying on the shingle carefully coiled to prevent it from getting tangled as it was pulled away. Fish always seem to be just a little further out than can be reached, so our fisherman looked around for a way to increase the distance he could hurl the stone and bait. Using a forked stick cut from a hedgerow, he found that he had a way of extending the arc through which the stone had to be swung to go faster and further. Thus, the casting stick was born and, with practice, increased casting distances brought more fish. All we have done, with the modern rod, reel and line, is to increase the distance we can cast, storing the line on a contraption that also allows us to control its flow, while introducing the feel of the vibrations on the line as the fish struggles to free itself.

We have stopped using a stone as a weight for casting. Now our leads have the right shape to cut through the air, giving even more distance. Since they are smaller in size for the same weight, the lead holds the bottom better. When tides are at their strongest we do not have to use much larger weights. All we do is to use a lead with grip wires built into it that pull more securely into the sea bed. We also have nylon lines, fine in diameter and incredibly strong. These are now used everywhere.

There are three types of reel available to the shore fisherman. The fixed-spool used by most freshwater anglers is both convenient to use and free from the control problems found when using the multiplier or centrepin. It has the possibility of changing spools, which means that a fisherman can carry several breaking strains of nylon, although only needing one reel body. The drawback with this reel is that in sizes suitable for sea fishing, where quite heavy lines are called for, the reel becomes too bulky. The multiplying reel is smaller and generally carries more line. Unfortunately, it is essential to practice with a multiplier before you can cast a bait with it effectively.

The centre-pin finds favour in certain areas. In Yorkshire and along the north-east coast, you will find many anglers equipped with a large drum reel. They use it because it has tremendous strength and can give a fast rate of retrieve when reeling the lead and line back. Off the rocky shores of that part of Britain there are huge, underwater jungles of thick seaweed. To land a hooked fish, or just to get

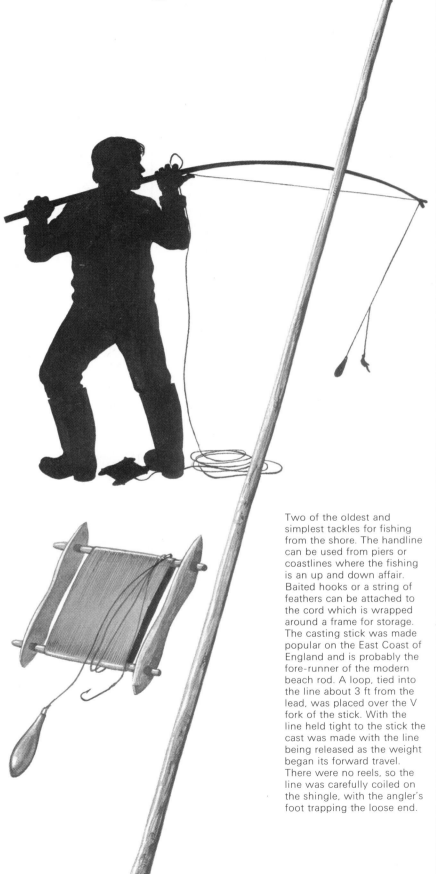

Two of the oldest and simplest tackles for fishing from the shore. The handline can be used from piers or coastlines where the fishing is an up and down affair. Baited hooks or a string of feathers can be attached to the cord which is wrapped around a frame for storage. The casting stick was made popular on the East Coast of England and is probably the fore-runner of the modern beach rod. A loop, tied into the line about 3 ft from the lead, was placed over the V fork of the stick. With the line held tight to the stick the cast was made with the line being released as the weight began its forward travel. There were no reels, so the line was carefully coiled on the shingle, with the angler's foot trapping the loose end.

64

the terminal tackle back to inspect the bait, is a struggle as the lead or fish has to be hauled through a mass of fronds that would easily break the average beach fisherman's gear. I would say the centre-pin reel was a special reel for localized purposes and more than a little difficult to learn to cast with.

When looking for reels for beach work ask yourself these questions:

1. Is it as small as possible? Big reels are harder to control, heavier and cost more.

2. Is it easy to take apart: does it have a spare spool? Changing lines at night in the cold is difficult enough with a take-apart reel. Struggling with half a dozen screws or reloading the only spool you have is a nightmare!

3. Will spare parts be easily available?

4. Will it fit your rod?

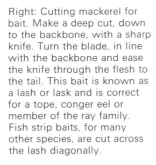

Right: Cutting mackerel for bait. Make a deep cut, down to the backbone, with a sharp knife. Turn the blade, in line with the backbone and ease the knife through the flesh to the tail. This bait is known as a lash or lask and is correct for a tope, conger eel or member of the ray family. Fish strip baits, for many other species, are cut across the lash diagonally.

Left: A modern beach rod suitable for casting weights of 3 to 6 oz. It has two equal sections, formed from hollow fibre glass tubes, joined by a glass spigot joint. The reel is a multipler, although a fixed-spool would be equally as good in use.

The shore angler's basic tackle

Shore fishing terminal rigs should be kept simple in construction. Inevitably, the angler will lose some tackle. It will either become caught up in rocky ground or be broken off from the reel line when a bad cast is made. Any over-complication of the rig will only cost time and money when a loss happens.

A rod is designed to do two things – to cast out the lead and to play out a fish. Because sea angling weights are much heavier than those used in freshwater, our rods tend to be stronger in construction to absorb the strains of casting and recovering a weight that may be entangled in underwater debris. Shore fishing rods spend most of their working lives casting. Very little time is spent in landing fish.

Two basic rods have grown out of the sport. There is an all-rounder, casting leads 3–5 ounces, any length from 10–12 feet. This rod will cope with many of our types of shore fishing that involve casting. Then we have a much heavier, more powerful version that is manufactured to throw weights of 6–8 ounces. Built for the heavy fishing of winter, when tides and currents are often at their strongest, or to cope with those big fish that venture inshore, this rod will measure between 11 and 13 feet in length.

Although constructed from hollow, fibreglass tubes, modern sea rods are still fairly heavy. Because of this, the lighter of the two types of rod is favoured by those anglers that are prepared to hold their rods in the hand throughout the fishing day, only laying them down to bait up or change rigs. The heavy rod, used by most cod fishermen, is often placed upright in a rod rest.

Assuming that we will, like most shore anglers, use a fixed-spool, it will have to be loaded with nylon. Balanced to the light casting rod, line of 15–18 lb breaking strain will suit very well. The heavier rod will call for lines of 18–25 lbs. The line should be wound onto the spool evenly to a point $\frac{1}{8}$ of an inch below the rim of the spool. Then a casting shock leader, one and a half rod lengths of stronger nylon, is tied to the loose end of the reel line. This leader absorbs the initial shock of the angler's casting action and is essential in preventing leads from flying off the line if a faulty cast is made.

The fishing terminal tackle can be a simple nylon paternoster with one or two hooks or a basic leger rig. These are joined to the casting leader using a split link or a strong swivel. Another split link serves to attach the casting weight.

66

Left: The casting leader knot is best for attaching your reel line to a length of heavier gauge nylon that will absorb the shock load of casting.

Above: Blood loops are useful to form hook droppers or links. Remember to lick the nylon before pulling the knot tight. This lubricates the coils, preventing line chafe.

Above: The double-blood knot is used to join two lengths of nylon which have reasonably similar diameters.

Above: Hook droppers may need a loop tied into the connecting terminal tackle. This 'Overhand' knot will do the job.

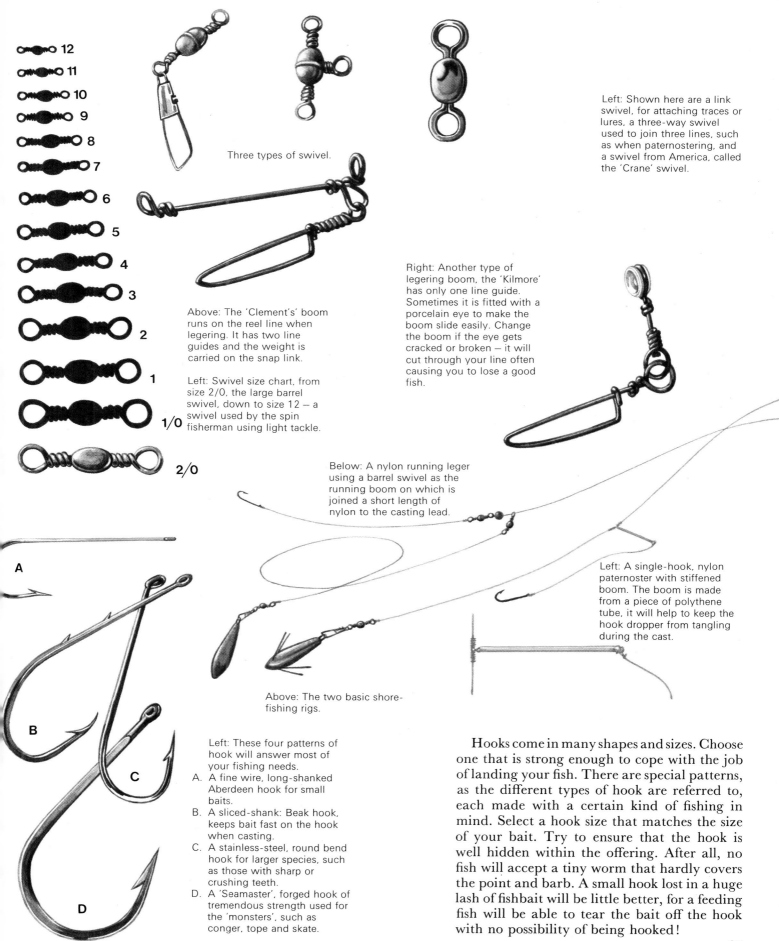

Three types of swivel.

Left: Shown here are a link swivel, for attaching traces or lures, a three-way swivel used to join three lines, such as when paternostering, and a swivel from America, called the 'Crane' swivel.

12
11
10
9
8
7
6
5
4
3
2
1
1/0
2/0

Above: The 'Clement's' boom runs on the reel line when legering. It has two line guides and the weight is carried on the snap link.

Left: Swivel size chart, from size 2/0, the large barrel swivel, down to size 12 — a swivel used by the spin fisherman using light tackle.

Right: Another type of legering boom, the 'Kilmore' has only one line guide. Sometimes it is fitted with a porcelain eye to make the boom slide easily. Change the boom if the eye gets cracked or broken — it will cut through your line often causing you to lose a good fish.

Below: A nylon running leger using a barrel swivel as the running boom on which is joined a short length of nylon to the casting lead.

Left: A single-hook, nylon paternoster with stiffened boom. The boom is made from a piece of polythene tube, it will help to keep the hook dropper from tangling during the cast.

A

B

C

D

Above: The two basic shore-fishing rigs.

Left: These four patterns of hook will answer most of your fishing needs.
A. A fine wire, long-shanked Aberdeen hook for small baits.
B. A sliced-shank: Beak hook, keeps bait fast on the hook when casting.
C. A stainless-steel, round bend hook for larger species, such as those with sharp or crushing teeth.
D. A 'Seamaster', forged hook of tremendous strength used for the 'monsters', such as conger, tope and skate.

Hooks come in many shapes and sizes. Choose one that is strong enough to cope with the job of landing your fish. There are special patterns, as the different types of hook are referred to, each made with a certain kind of fishing in mind. Select a hook size that matches the size of your bait. Try to ensure that the hook is well hidden within the offering. After all, no fish will accept a tiny worm that hardly covers the point and barb. A small hook lost in a huge lash of fishbait will be little better, for a feeding fish will be able to tear the bait off the hook with no possibility of being hooked!

Casting from the shore

Take a walk along any beach where anglers fish regularly and you will see many styles of casting, ranging from the exaggerated tournament cast intended to throw leads over the magic 200 yards to the short, stunted, action of the man who holds the rod over his head producing the quick flip that can throw the lead no more than 50 yards. Between these two styles there is the average cast for the average angler. Only practice, developing smoothness and exact timing, will produce an effortless cast every time. There is a style of shore-casting that is right for most people to begin with. Called the 'layback cast', it was introduced to the sea anglers of Britain by Leslie Moncrieff in the early 1960s.

Leslie Moncrieff is one of the finest casters and teachers of casting. After a lifetime of shore fishing and watching the struggles of novices, he set out to put his cast across to the angling world. He reasoned that complete beginners to the sport required a simple action and a cast that could be extended in the time that it took to build up the power in the rod. This would smooth out the whole performance.

Ideally, a beginner to shorefishing should seek the advice of someone who has had experience of this branch of angling. Of course, you cannot learn to cast without a rod but knowing which rod to buy is difficult. By seeking advice and by being able to start practicing with a number of other people's rods, you will get the feel of the casting action. Your friends will be able to assess your ability to handle a particular length and weight of rod. Your own body strength will dictate the kind of rod that you are best able to handle.

From the step-by-step illustration of the "layback cast" we see that the rod is swung in

an arc. As the caster swivels round from the hips his body moves ahead of the rod. The lead, as a dead weight, holds back the natural tendency for the rod to straighten. When about two thirds of the cast is accomplished, the power built up in the rod begins to assert itself. The tip speeds forward with progressive acceleration, straightening the rod blank, which springs the lead onto its forward trajectory. Laying back into the cast with a leaning forward into the follow-through produces a lengthened but much smoother casting action.

The position of your feet and hands is important. With the correct lead for the rod, adopt the casting position. This will help you to get to know the feel of a loaded fishing rod.

Practise the casting action by slowly moving through the cast without releasing the lead.

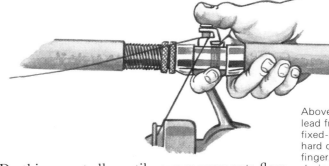

Do this repeatedly until your movements flow smoothly. Now you are ready to begin casting in earnest. Choose a big, empty, field away from human habitation and farm animals. There is a real danger in "cracking" leads off the line when learning to cast. Always use a casting leader of heavy gauge nylon and do not take an audience with you. We all make mistakes when learning, but to have someone watching your faltering first efforts leads to

Above: Casting a heavy lead from a rod with a fixed-spool reel can be hard on your index finger. The Thumbutton device makes casting a lot easier. Line is lifted from the spool and trapped under the shaped thumb device. As the cast is made, the thumb is lifted from the button at the moment when you wish to release the lead — easy casting without removing skin from your finger!

A slab-sided torpedo.

The 'Sandfast' lead, that will grip in all but the fastest tides.

A 'Breakaway' lead (above and below) that will hold in most tides.

Above: Leads for the shorecaster.

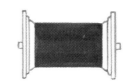

Above: Never load too much line onto your multiplying reel. Wind on the nylon to a point $\frac{1}{4}$ in down from the rim of the spool.

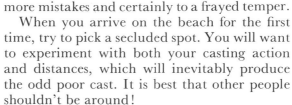

Above: Bass from the shingle at Dungeness. Though widely known as a winter cod fishing venue, Dungeness now produces some fair bass because of the warm water that flows into the sea from the nuclear power station.

An easily constructed beach rest, made by lashing 4-ft lengths of wooden battens together.

more mistakes and certainly to a frayed temper.

When you arrive on the beach for the first time, try to pick a secluded spot. You will want to experiment with both your casting action and distances, which will inevitably produce the odd poor cast. It is best that other people shouldn't be around!

Left: The smooth but simple 'layback' cast for fishing from the shore. Either a multiplying or fixed-spool reel can be used.

69

Cod and whiting from beaches

With the arrival of autumn's first frost, shore anglers begin to think of cod and whiting, both species which thrive in the cold northerly seas. The whiting comes first, generally about the first week in October. From the shore we can expect whiting weighing about a pound each. Later in the autumn there are bigger fish off our coasts, called channel whiting. These grow to 3 pounds or more but they rarely come into the very shallow water. Later in October the shore fisherman expects cod – big fish from Arctic seas – that follow whiting and sprat shoals down through the North Sea and into the English Channel. There are times when the biggest of these cod, fish of 30 pounds or more, can be hooked within 50 yards of the shingle.

The whiting can be feeding down the coastal areas in huge shoals. Often there are so many fish that we hook them two at a time as they rob the hooks we have baited for cod! The bite from the small whiting is unmistakable, a rattling pull at the rod tip as the fish attempts to tear the worms from the hook. They will take fairly large hooks and make a mess of the hook snoods with their tiny, sharp teeth. It is possible that you will hook a whiting and begin to reel it in when the line goes solid, as if it has fouled a heavy rock or bunch of weed. Do not pull wildly on the gear, because a cod may have taken your hooked whiting.

We do not often use a small whiting as a cast bait as it is difficult to achieve any casting distance owing to wind resistance on the bait. Most autumn and winter anglers use the lugworm or a mixture of worm and shellfish, such as mussel. These baits cast well and are taken by a wide variety of fish species. Try to thread your worms onto the hook, building up an attractive cod-sized mouthful while hiding the metal of the hook. A simple nylon two-hook paternoster is the rig to use with hooks size 6/0 for cod or 2/0 for whiting.

Using small hooks can be an advantage since other winter fish, such as dabs, can take the bait. They are often reeled in after the hook-baits have been left to await the arrival of a cod. These small flatfish are in fine condition in the cold months of the year, although on cod tackle they cannot be expected to put up much of a fight.

Hooking and playing a cod from the shore is not without thrills and problems. The fight can be a heavy, arm-aching affair. This is not because the cod is famed as a fighter but because it can lie in the tide, using the power of the

Above: The cod is a greedy fellow with a keen appetite for lugworm baits.

Right: Lugworm. The best known of the roving worms, the lugworm lives on sandy and muddy shores below the high water mark. The presence of lugworm can be easily detected by the worm-like twists of sand cast up on the surface. There will also be a number of small blow-holes within a short distance of the casts. The lugworm lives by swallowing large quantities of sand, which it passes through its body extracting the nutrients as it does so. Try to hide the hook within the body of the worm leaving the point and barb exposed.

Right: Ragworm. There are several species of this marine worm. Basically they differ only in size and in where they are found. The common ragworm is found living in the mud that accumulates at the bottom of harbours. Some species are fond of the areas of slow-running water found at the mouth of rivers and saltwater creeks. Another fruitful hunting ground for the bait gatherer is among weeds and small rocks between the tidelines.

Right: Cockles. These very common shellfish can be gathered by raking in sandy and mud beaches. There are several species, but all are useful as bait. They can be used as a fresh bait or cooked before use.

heavy water to place a great strain on the end tackle. The cod often comes to the beach with its mouth gaping wide. The press of water into the mouth adds a lot to the strain in fighting the fish.

Many cod are lost to the fisherman within 10 yards of the shingle. This happens when the fish is on a tight line as it is played in. Then, at the water's edge, we meet conditions of rough water where the waves turn over. If a wave picks the fish up it can momentarily release the line pressure, the fish drops back to be pulled up with a jerk into a tight line once more. This causes a break at the hook line or at the leader knot. Be careful as the fish nears the beach. With the line kept taut, wait for a wave that will beach your fish on the shingle. Then move smartly, take hold of the casting leader and drag the cod clear of the inshore surge.

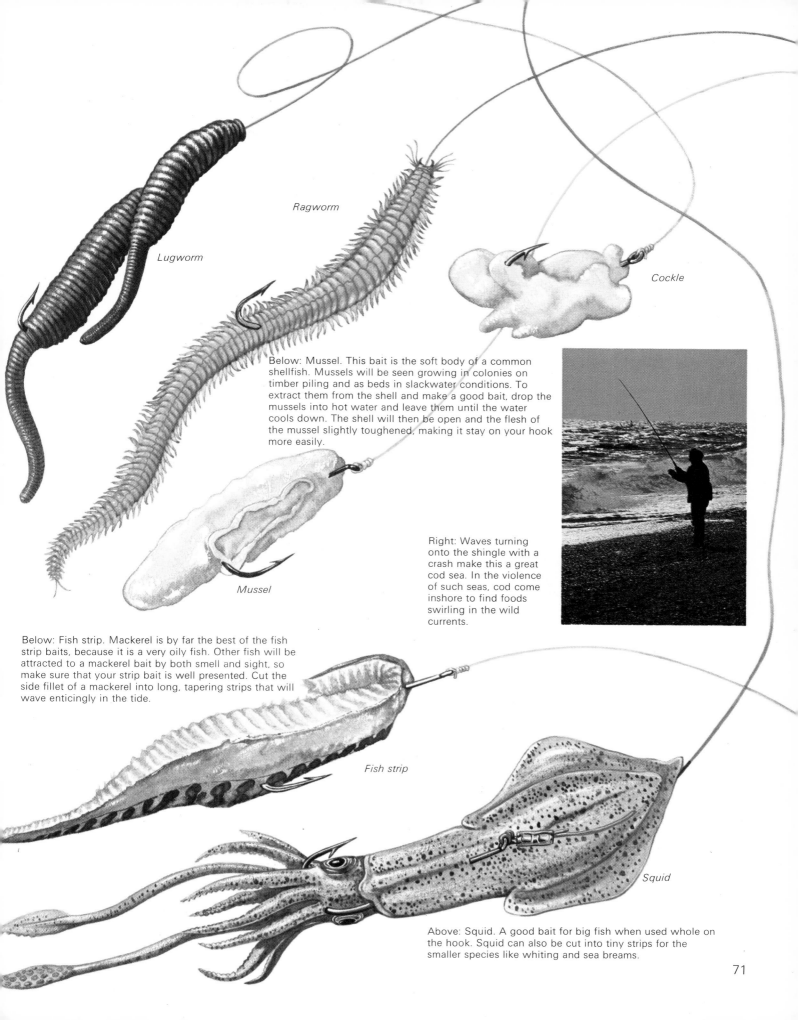

Lugworm

Ragworm

Cockle

Below: Mussel. This bait is the soft body of a common shellfish. Mussels will be seen growing in colonies on timber piling and as beds in slackwater conditions. To extract them from the shell and make a good bait, drop the mussels into hot water and leave them until the water cools down. The shell will then be open and the flesh of the mussel slightly toughened, making it stay on your hook more easily.

Mussel

Right: Waves turning onto the shingle with a crash make this a great cod sea. In the violence of such seas, cod come inshore to find foods swirling in the wild currents.

Below: Fish strip. Mackerel is by far the best of the fish strip baits, because it is a very oily fish. Other fish will be attracted to a mackerel bait by both smell and sight, so make sure that your strip bait is well presented. Cut the side fillet of a mackerel into long, tapering strips that will wave enticingly in the tide.

Fish strip

Squid

Above: Squid. A good bait for big fish when used whole on the hook. Squid can also be cut into tiny strips for the smaller species like whiting and sea breams.

Fishing the sandy beaches

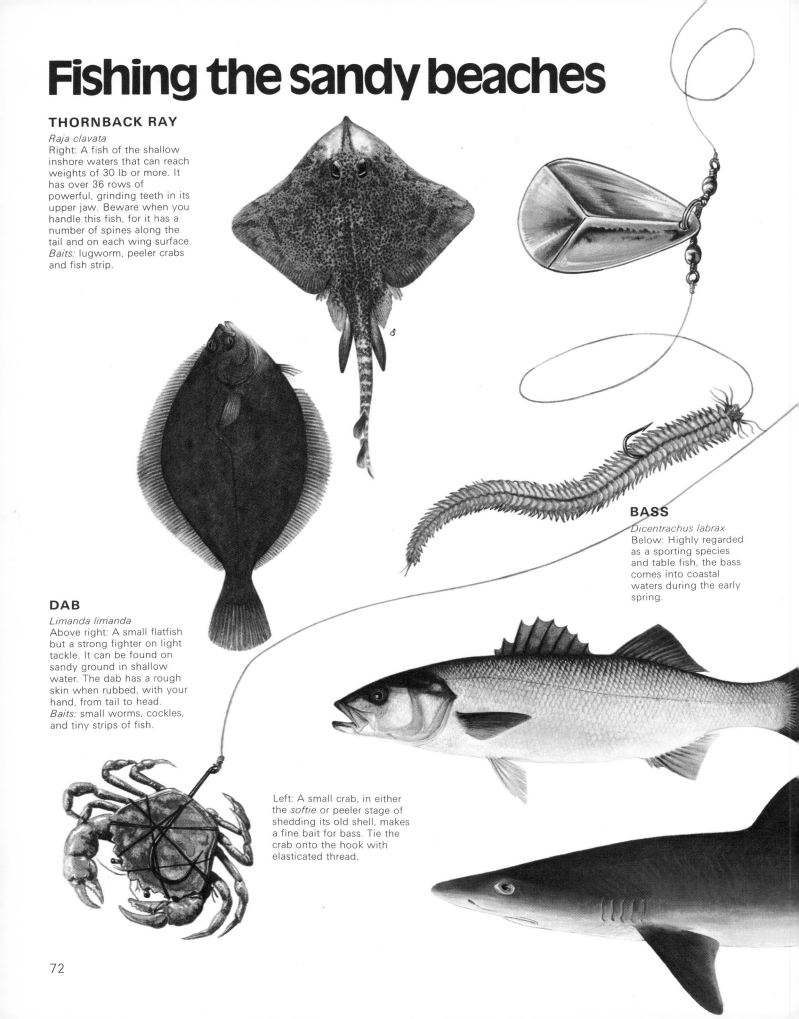

THORNBACK RAY

Raja clavata
Right: A fish of the shallow inshore waters that can reach weights of 30 lb or more. It has over 36 rows of powerful, grinding teeth in its upper jaw. Beware when you handle this fish, for it has a number of spines along the tail and on each wing surface.
Baits: lugworm, peeler crabs and fish strip.

DAB

Limanda limanda
Above right: A small flatfish but a strong fighter on light tackle. It can be found on sandy ground in shallow water. The dab has a rough skin when rubbed, with your hand, from tail to head.
Baits: small worms, cockles, and tiny strips of fish.

BASS

Dicentrachus labrax
Below: Highly regarded as a sporting species and table fish, the bass comes into coastal waters during the early spring.

Left: A small crab, in either the *softie* or peeler stage of shedding its old shell, makes a fine bait for bass. Tie the crab onto the hook with elasticated thread.

Left: Many fish can be attracted to feed by incorporating a spoon within the rig. The baited spoon will take flounders, plaice and other flatfish. Fished as a paternoster, a baited spoon can produce good catches of cod and haddock.

Right: A thornback ray caught from a patch of sandy ground in a rocky cove. The fish took a bunch of lugworm intended for marauding bass.

The word bass conjures up visions of creaming breakers, turning with wind-blown crests to spill over, sending even-depthed tables of water shooting up onto golden, sandy beaches. The angler who seeks bass must travel to the west-facing Atlantic surf beaches of Europe. There are bass swimming in other areas of our islands but on the surf strand the bass angler feels in tune with this powerful sea perch. The attraction for anglers is environmental. They wade out into the surf to cast, even staying in the water with the surge repeatedly running up past them.

Successful bass fishing calls for dedication. The ability to cast a good distance is vital and so is the desire to hold the rod throughout the fishing day, for few bass will be caught by the fisherman who leaves his rod in a rod rest. The bass run backwards and forwards along the length of the breakers searching for worms and sandeels forced out of the sand as the waves smash onto the beach. Sometimes the fish are about three or four breakers out from the beach, although they can often be seen flashing through the quiet, even tables of water that pass up the beach beyond the angler's waders.

Providing the surf is not as mountainous as can sometimes be produced by an offshore storm, there will be little weed drifting in the water. This loosening of bottom-growing weed during severe storms can be the curse of the bass angler. The weed swills around in the breakers, gathering in bunches on the line and hooks, preventing any chance of a bass finding the bait or a bite being detected if a fish does happen along. During the quiet spells, when far-off ocean winds are still, the height of the surf drops and other fish come into the shallow water. Flounders are particularly fond of the feeding conditions prevailing on a bass strand. after leaving the rivers and estuaries on the spawning migration.

With calm conditions giving just a gentle swell that turns softly over, we find predators coming into casting range. Late in the evening, as the sun sinks, tope swim into the bass beach looking for food. They are probably searching for flounders lying half-covered in the sand. The best fishing time is on a making tide into the night. Tope, rays and monkfish can be found during the warmer months, sometimes grabbing a bait intended for bass but rarely biting during the hours of daylight. A wired leger trace is essential and mackerel lashes are the best bait.

If you intend fishing for these species, arm yourself with the necessary means of removing the hook from their mouths. Pliers with a sharp cutting edge will remove the hook or cut the wire trace. A lamp of some sort is essential when tanging with these fish in shallow water and on the sand. Since the rod is rarely held when night fishing, bite detections present a problem. Either put the rod in a rest with the reel out of gear, with ratchet on, or slacken the reel drag down to a minimum and shine the lamp onto the rod tip. A white painted section below the tip ring will aid night vision and there is even a battery-less, glowing, bite indicator that can be fixed to the top of your rod if you prefer a sophisticated tell-tale, but for beginners this is probably unnecessary.

TOPE

Galeorhinus galeus
Below: A live-bearing member of the shark family, the tope is truly a sportsman's fish. It comes into shallow beaches and estuaries searching for food, which can be immature fish of all kinds. The teeth of the tope are incredibly sharp so wire traces are necessary. *Baits:* Most fish baits, but mackerel and herring are best.

Tackle for sandy beach species

A good bass rod has to be light in the hand, for holding over long periods, capable of casting leads of between 2–4 ounces. But it must also be tough enough to pull in large bunches of seaweed or the occasional heavy fish. The rod should be 10 to 11 feet long and should have an adequate number of rings to support the line along the length of the rod. Whether the handle is fully corked or fitted with small handle sections is your choice. I like to feel cork under my hands. Cork does not get slippery like the plastic handles.

Either a multiplier or a fixed-spool reel will cope with all your light tackle fishing on the bass beach. Playing a fish from a fixed spool reel is not as satisfying as a multipler, because the line has to pull around a right angle formed by the bale arm and, of course, it is more difficult to control the running off of line from the fixed spool. With both reels a line of 12–18 lb breaking strain will be correct, providing the reel line is joined to a casting leader of 25–20 lb B.S. Join your end tackles, whether paternoster or leger rigs, to the casting leader, using a quality swivel or a split link. Remember to give the end rig a test pull just in case there are any weaknesses that would be sure to show up when playing a good fish.

Baits for the species known to frequent the sandy beach are of great variety. Worms, both lug and ragworm, are perfect hookbaits. They are easily placed onto the hooks and should be threaded on with the worm being led over the point of the hook and gently pushed up to the hook eye. There is some advantage in using more than one worm, particularly if your worms are small, to provide an attractive bait for a marauding fish in the shallow water. Bass, flounders and dogfish will accept worm baits but when the larger predators move in, our thoughts on bait and end tackles must alter. The tope, a near relative of the true shark, has a mouthful of sharp teeth and a tough skin that can easily rip through a nylon hook link. You must use wire, either as a supple, cable-laid trace or as a short length of wire connected to the hook to which you join a strong piece of casting leader of about 60–80 lb B.S. nylon. Rays – and the possibility of hooking a monk-fish when shorefishing – will demand a shorter length of wire leader between the bait and lead link.

Flounders are a species of flatfish that can often be taken from the sandy shore. They spend a part of each season in estuaries and high up

Right: The simplest of nylon paternoster rigs for shore fishermen. Tie in two blood loops 12 and 30 in up from the lead. These are cut on one side of the loop to form hook droppers.

Below: A wire, running leger rig, ideal for tope fishing from the beach. The wire is made fast with crimped ferrules – standard knots would come undone when a severe strain is applied to the rig.

Right: A useful addition to the flatfish rig; a flounder spoon will act as an attractor. When reeled slowly towards the rod, the spoon blade lifts little spurts of sand which flounders will investigate as they continually search for their food.

Right, opposite page: A typical bass or light tackle beachcasting rod. The multiplying reel shown is one of the few available for left-hand winding.

Top left: A very famous shore fisherman, Leslie Moncrieff, fishes the surf at Stradbally Strand, Dingle Peninsula, Co. Kerry. Top right: a difficult time as a bass splashes in the water at the angler's feet. Bottom left: Bass are becoming a rare species in some areas, so release unwanted fish to the sea. Bottom right: Anglers fishing an open Atlantic bass beach in the West of Ireland. Fish of 2 to 3 lbs are the average size taken, with the months of April to October providing the best shorefishing.

into tidal rivers feeding on the lush growth of marsh vegetation and on the minute creatures that live within the weeds. These flatfish leave the rivers in January, and sometimes later, to spawn. They will then feed in the inshore waters, where the flounder regains its strength, before returning to the estuaries. Flounders will take baits intended for bass. They will even take a bass-size bait and hook, although this fish needs a little longer time in which to seize the bait. Fish for your flounder with a single lugworm on a long-shanked hook. About size No. 2 is correct, both to mount the worm bait and to enable gripping the hook to remove it.

The flounder is a humble fish: perhaps familiarity makes them so, for many fishermen catch them by accident. But to many anglers the flounder is a cornerstone of sea fishing.

Fishing from the rocky shore

The powerful actions of wind and tide, over millions of years, have given us two distinct types of rocky shore. There are stretches of European coastline where massive cliffs fall vertically into the sea with deep water right up to the foot of the rock faces. There are also places where the foreshore is composed of broken rock mixed up with patches of sand and mud. In these places there may be cliffs rising behind the beach but generally they will stand back from the shore. Over the years rocks will have broken away from the cliffs to roll into the water. The different shore structures present different problems to the angler.

You can use a wider variety of angling methods on a rock mark with deep water close in to the cliffs. Depending on the fish species that live below the waves, you can float fish, spin and cast out legered baits. There can be large fish right under the angler's feet. Conger eels will live within the broken ground at the base of rock ledges. Ballan wrasse can find a hole or crevice in which to hide while pollack and rock codling will be attracted by the many creatures that live in this environment. Many species of migratory fish, such as mackerel in the summer and coalfish in the winter, will be brought within the angler's casting range because there is deep water at all times.

When fishing from the rocks, you need to keep a watchful eye for the sea condition. Even on fairly calm days there could be a swell running into the cliffs. Be alert for the occasional wave that is larger and more powerful as it surges up the cliff base. Anglers can be swept off their platforms to be carried away by the backsurge. Once in the water it can be difficult to get back to safety. Check on the state of the tide before climbing onto ledges. Make sure that there is a way back as the tide comes in!

Fishing the rocky shore where there are broken boulders and fingers of rock jutting out into the sea can be hard on the tackle box. If the sea is shallow it is pretty certain that there will be many outcrops of rock and attached weed that you cannot see. You will need bait-

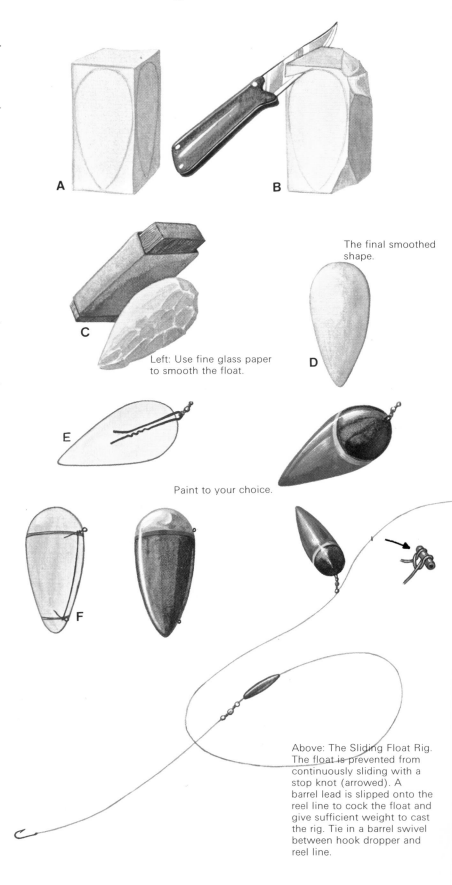

The final smoothed shape.

Left: Use fine glass paper to smooth the float.

Paint to your choice.

Above right: Making a sea float. Buy a small piece of 1-in square balsa wood. Draw a pear shape on all four sides of a 4-in section (A). Shape the wood, taking care not to cut your fingers (B). Roughly shape the float, which can be smoothed with fine glass paper (C and D). Drill a hole and glue in a hairgrip and swivel (E). An alternative fixing for the line guides is to twist a wire, forming two eyelets, which is then bound onto the float (F). A smear of waterproof glue will make both methods of fixing guides permanent.

Above: The Sliding Float Rig. The float is prevented from continuously sliding with a stop knot (arrowed). A barrel lead is slipped onto the reel line to cock the float and give sufficient weight to cast the rig. Tie in a barrel swivel between hook dropper and reel line.

Four spinning lures for the rock fisherman.

A. A 'Redgill', possibly the most successful of the modern baits.

B. A French lure, the 'Mak', very popular with mackerel anglers.

C. A traditional rubber eel, made from highly-colourful gas tube with a long-shanked hook that has been bent to make the lure swerve in the water.

D. The finest of the bar spoons, a 'German Sprat', that simulates the motion of a sandeel as it is retrieved.

casting tackle to get the terminal rigs out to where fish are. Tackle will become tangled in the broken bottom, for the lead always seems to find its way into gaps in the rocks.

Fish are always likely to be here so you must come to terms with the hazards. Fish a weak link to the lead, a piece of nylon that is of lower breaking strain than the main line. Collect a number of spare weights that you don't mind losing – old sparking plugs, heavy nuts and bolts are all useful.

Shallow water means good light down to the seabed. Providing the shore is not too exposed to heavy weather there will be a plentiful growth of weeds into which a vast number of minute animals will crawl. These small creatures are the natural food of many fish species who will come in on the rising tide to feed. Where there are shellfish, such as mussels, there will be plaice. Mud and sand patches will hold different kinds of marine worms and, as the small fish forage for tiny animals, they will be chased by even larger fish. Predatory fish, like tope and the many sorts of dogfish also visit these rich feeding areas.

Inspect the fishing area first. At low spring tides, you will see where natural hazards are. Your inspection must be thorough. Find where the open patches of sand are, especially those that lie between clumps of rock and weed.

Above: With a little help, this small lad lands his first wrasse.

Below: Three natural baits for the rock fisherman.

Mussel can be gathered from beds, uncovered by the receding tide or gathered from pier piling and harbour walls.

Crabs, at the peeler or soft stage of their lives, are a perfect bait for bass and flounders in particular but will be taken, greedily, by many fish off the rocks.

The limpet, which is found living on exposed rocky shores, makes a good bait for the ballan wrasse.

Fish of the rocky shore

The number of fish species that haunt the rocky shore is countless. They range from the massive conger eel to the tiniest goby, found hiding under stones in rockpools left as the tide ebbs away. Not all of the fish are of interest to the serious angler who wants to catch something to eat. Newcomers to the rocky shore might be forgiven for becoming frightened by some of the fish. There are fish with sharp spines called sea scorpions, others with a casing of what looks like armour plating, wildly coloured in vivid reds, blue and grey. These fish are gurnards, striking to look at but harmless. The rocklings are slender fish belonging to the cod family. They have a number of barbules sprouting from their jaws. Counting the barbules will help you to identify the species.

Wherever you find rocky shores, with attached seaweeds and shellfish of the barnacle or limpet kind, you can expect to catch wrasse. The common fish inshore is the ballan wrasse, a fish which looks rather like a freshwater carp. It has beautiful scales and a variety of colouring. The body colour is to some extent adapted to the colours found in the habitat in which it lives. These inshore fish are able to pick limpets off the rock with their teeth – a considerable achievement. The cuckoo wrasse will venture close to the cliffs if there is deep water below them. This species has different colouring for males and females which has confused people into thinking that they are two separate species of wrasse.

Pollack, especially the smaller ones, will live under the cliffs. Swimming high in the water, pollack chase the smaller fish and are taken on fish strips or artificial lures that spin or wobble. The flashing silver spoon is probably the best pollack lure, closely followed by the many varieties of rubber or plastic artificial sandeels. You can catch cod, or rather codling, from the rocks. Sometimes they are a deep red colour which seems to give them a camouflaged effect as they swim between the kelp fronds. These fish will go to feed in far-off waters when they have grown to a couple of pounds in weight. Then they change their colouring to the yellow-green of the deep sea cod.

Mackerel shoals visit our shores during the summer months. You will know that the mackerel "are in" because they are visible to anglers and other people who watch all that happens out to sea. The shoals move speedily across the inshore waters, chasing the fry of many species. As they swim, their dorsal fins carve through the waves disturbing the surface.

The mackerel are our principal bait fish. Most anglers use them for bait, either as strips or whole lashes to catch big specimens like tope and rays. From the rocks, the mackerel makes a good bait for cod, ling, conger and pollack. Mackerel are best caught by spinning a simple bar spoon or casting a three-feathered string of hooks with a paternostered weight. Let the feathers sink down below the waves, then work the feathers back in a sink-and-draw motion. Do not take more mackerel than you need.

BALLAN WRASSE

Labrus bergylta
Below: The ballan wrasse is truly a shore fisher's species. It lives in rocky, broken ground on reefs and at the base of sea cliffs. It may be a variety of colours from brilliant orange to vivid green. Strong teeth enable it to gather limpets from the inter-tidal zone. *Baits:* crustaceans and small marine worms.

CONGER EEL

Conger conger
Above: One of the toughest of fighters, the conger eel lives in rocky ground, harbour walls and within sunken wrecks. It can grow over 100 lbs in weight but a shore-caught conger of 30 lbs is considered good. Use wired-traces and forged hooks for this fish and beware of the vicious teeth. *Baits:* whole fish or fish strips.

Above: The shore fisher's spinning rod. 8-ft long, it is used with either a fixed spool or multiplying reel. This kind of rod also allows you to float fish from rocky shores. Spinning is hard on a rod, so inspect whippings and rings regularly.

POLLACK

Pollachius pollachius
Right: The pollack is a member of the cod family that favours rocky ground, reefs and wrecks. It has a curved lateral line, whereas the coalfish, with which it is often confused, has a straight, white lateral line. Its bottom jaw extends well beyond its upper jaw. *Baits:* worms, shellfish, fish strip and most spinning lures.

MACKEREL

Scomber scombrus
Right: One of the fastest and strongest fighters in the sea when fished for on the correct tackle, yet most sea anglers only know the fish as a bait! The best fun in mackerel fishing is to use a small spinning lure on an ultralight trout rod.
Baits: tiny slips of fish, feathered lures and spinners.

A. Left: The traditional mackerel spinner. Made to troll behind a boat, it has no in-built weight so needs a spinning lead to enable you to cast it. The coloured tassel is not always incorporated by the manufacturer but can make all the difference!

B. Above: A whirling blade lure, the Vibro. This is a useful spinning lure for most species.

C. Below: The coarse fisherman's plug lure. Even this can be used to effect when sea spinning. Pollack will rise, from an underwater reef, to slash at it as it floats. Keep the plug small; light colours with a touch of red are favourite.

D. Left: A basic spinning trace. The reel line is tied to a swivel, above which is fixed a spiral lead that is heavy enough to cast and sink the rubber eel. A bend in the lead will give it anti-kink properties. Use a lure trace, in nylon, of about 3 ft.

79

Spinning from the rocks

Spinning an artificial lure is an art. This particular form of angling is also wrongly named, for not all lures spin. Some wobble from side to side while others achieve a fish-catching action by having either fins or a tail that move as the lure is reeled back to the angler. I prefer to call this type of angling "working a bait" and you really will be working, covering the water in both depth and distance to find fish.

There is very little difference between the activities of freshwater or saltwater fishermen who spin or work a bait. I believe the sea angler has the better opportunity of sport because there are many more species that will take an artificial lure in the coastal waters of Europe. The tackle is fairly simple – a suitable rod, reel and line to which is tied any one of a number of lures. The chosen lure can be made from metal, plastic, rubber or wood. Using an artificial bait made of metal is the simplest method because it requires no lead in order to be able to cast it out. The other forms of lure will demand the attachment of sufficient weight both to cast them and sink them below the waves down to the waiting fish. The secret of successful spinning is to use the rod and reel in a way that gives an attractive motion to the lure as it is retrieved.

Simply casting out and reeling in a lure will not catch many fish. The lure has to be worked. This means that you cast, allow the bait to sink to where fish might be and then retrieve the lure in a series of movements of the rod tip, or differing speeds of winding on the reel handle, that will make the lure act like a frightened or injured fish. There are baits that have a proven fish-catching ability built into them, based on the current acting on the shape of the lure. This makes the metal or rubber object swerve in the water. It is always worth including a quality swivel into the spinning rig. Some lures do spin, which results in a degree of twist being introduced onto the reel line. An anti-kink lead will help, with the swivel, to keep twist to the minimum.

The shape of spinning leads is important. Use one that incurs little resistance to the passage of the tackle through the water. Make certain the weight is dull in colour. I have known fish to grab at a new and bright barrel lead. Place the lead weight at least one yard from the lure so that it will not dampen the action of the lure too much.

A spinning trace, the length of nylon between lure and swivel, is subjected to hard use during

Above: A unique situation for the shore angler. Close-in to a sandy beach there is a reef, the proximity of which ensures a ready supply of fish to the angler from the shore. The clear water demands that tackle and bait be presented in a life-like form.

a spinning session. It may be hauled around sharp rockfaces or dragged over shingle and sand, which will severely weaken the trace. Check its condition frequently or, better still, use a flexible wire trace which withstands the strain of fishing and also provides protection against the sharp teeth of species such as the ling. You can never tell which type of fish will follow and take a spun lure. All sea species are predatory by instinct and most of them will attempt to take a man-made bait that appears lifelike in its behaviour!

Left: Long fingers of broken reef extending from the shore, with patches of sandy ground between them. The water is shallow so fish move in with the rising tide.

Right: Deep water right under the angler's rod tip. Fish are present on all states of tide. Wrasse, pollack and conger can be taken from what is an ideal fishing platform of flat, evenly-stepped rock buttresses.

Below: Fishing among the rocks can be productive but keep control of the fish — never let them dive down into the weeds and broken ground.

Left: Take a look around you when fishing among the rocks. Many rockpools have a menagerie of minute creatures and beautiful coloured weeds, that are freshened by each high tide. Among the weeds you can find many hookbaits.

Left: Wrasse have sharp spines on the dorsal fin, so hold the fish firmly, folding the fin flat when extracting your hook.

The complete shorefisher

It is possible to fish from the shore line in all weathers. The seasons are dictated by the fish. Providing you can get close to the water you can usually fish but care must be taken when seas break onto the rocks or run fiercely up onto sand beach and shingle shore. The mighty wave that batters you onto your heels has a backsurge that can sweep anybody off their feet and out into the inshore spoil from which there is little chance of rescue. Have respect for the sea at all times. It can be hard on the unwary!

Personal safety should be followed by protection. Wear the right clothes and boots for the places and weather you are fishing in. A number of layers of underclothing with two woollen sweaters will keep out the cold when covered overall by a jacket or smock and trousers that are both wind and waterproof. Remember, it is easy to take off clothing if you become too warm but difficult to keep warm without adequate gear.

Avoid slippery rocks. Algae-covered rocks give a good foothold when dry but become treacherous when the tide drives spray up over them. When fishing the beaches do not wade our too far. You will not improve your distance cast by wading waist-deep into the surf. When you are out that far your casting action becomes cramped and hastened as the rollers sweep in and water presses against your legs. Better to stay in shallow water, relax into your style and get a good, un-hurried cast that will bring your distance.

Handling a big fish close-in to the shore is always a problem. Fish such as tope will swim in as they are played out but come suddenly alive when they realise that the water hardly covers their backs. Nevertheless, consider what you want of the fish before resorting to a gaff. If the species you have hooked is a sporting one offering little food value it is best to have a companion tail the fish ashore. Should you want to eat your fish, gaff it with a smooth, purposeful action. Then get it onto firm ground before attempting to remove the hook. Kill the fish quickly and cleanly with a sharp blow from a *priest*, which can be made from a short length of heavy metal pipe. Most round fish can be despatched by a blow across the head directly above the eyes. Do not leave your fish to flap around on the sand where it will die by suffocation.

Replace unwanted fish back into the water quickly after removing the hook. Skates, rays,

Left: Rubber eels are good artificial lures for many species. They are easy to make from a length of flexible gas piping into which is inserted a hook connected to a swivel by a spiral link.

Left: Mackerel are attracted to any lure that resembles a small fish. To catch mackerel for bait, anglers use feathers, which are a number of hooks with chicken feathers whipped onto the hook shanks. These can be easily made at home.

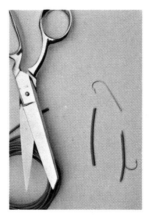

Left: Small artificial eels can be made by slipping small lengths of plastic tubing over the hook shank. These will catch mackerel. Alternate the eels with feathered hooks to make a choice of lure.

dogfish, conger and tope all have sharp teeth that must be avoided. The coarse fisherman's gag is of little use when handling these species, so use a block of hardwood placed into the mouth between the teeth. Obviously you will have to wait for the fish to open its mouth before inserting the block. Then the hook can be reached and removed with long-nosed pliers or strong forceps. Try not to leave a hook inside any fish that is to go back into the sea. Should the fish be damaged in any way, it is better to kill it humanely rather than let it die soon after its return.

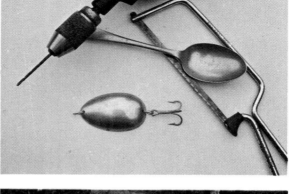

Left: Very efficient spoon lures can be made from old cutlery with the simplest of tools.

Left: The sea angler's tackle box. It is necessary for keeping all your tackle in a clean condition, away from the ravaging effect of salt water.

Above: Keeping dry and warm is very important. Begin with plenty of warm, woollen sweaters over which you can wear a jacket and trousers made of windproof material that is totally watertight! Your rubber boots should be covered by the trousers. A piece of towelling, around your neck, will keep out all but the worst weather.

Below: Removing a hook from a shark or tope is not a great problem. You need a block of hardwood, for the fish to bite on. This will prevent it closing its mouth on your hand or the cutting pliers. These are used to remove the hook or to cut the wire trace close to the hook.

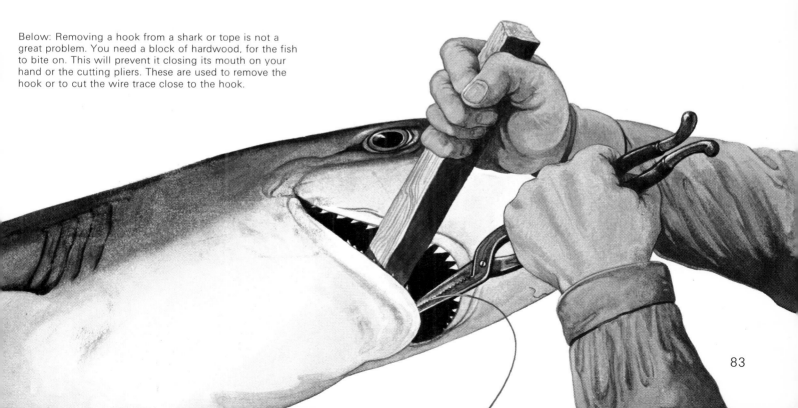

Fishing from piers and harbours

On any stretch of coastline we find some form of man-made refuge for boats. Sometimes the landing place will be just a small pier, reaching out from the shore into water deep enough to bring in small fishing boats. These will be rivalled by enormous harbour installations built to take the largest ocean-going merchant and passenger vessels. Whatever the size of harbour, it will attract both fish and anglers. The fish come to scavenge for food that has either been thrown into the water by people or for the smaller creatures, such as shellfish, that attach themselves to the piles and underwater structures. The anglers know of the attraction that this form of habitat has for fish but, more importantly, they know that piers and harbour walls extend their fishing range. The long arm of the harbour wall allows any angler to find deeper water than he could cast to from ordinary shore fishing locations.

High harbour structures and deep water spell danger to the unwary so you must be sure of your footing particularly when bad sea conditions send waves crashing against the sea wall. Take care and never act in an irresponsible fashion.

The fish species that you will encounter are fewer in number than could be expected from the rocky shore. This is because the amount and variety of food available to the fish is limited. Polluted harbour water, where oil and domestic waste are present, will spoil the living conditions of small animals and fish alike. On the other hand, fish offal that is created when trawlers gut fish after their return to harbour can be regarded as fish-attracting material. Fish will come to expect a feed along the harbour wall. So species like conger take to living in cracks in the walls, while mullet swim like dark torpedos under the boats' hulls. Pouting and small pollack will dart out from the cast shadows to grab at tiny morsels of offal. Occasionally big, scavenging bass visit the harbours to feed.

The mussels that drape themselves on wooden piling provide a constant source of feeding for many species of fish. At the same time the baulks of timber provide hiding places for the very small specimens that swim within the waving weed fronds.

Fishing from these places is similar in pattern to fishing from an inshore dinghy. There is little casting to do, it is more of an up-and-down fishing. Rods can be shorter, with either a fixed-spool reel or a multiplying reel. A simple

Right: A pier or *foul ground* paternoster. Tie in a short length of weak nylon below a swivel for attaching your weight. Should the lead become fast in the bottom you can break out the rig without losing it.

paternoster, perhaps with booms for the hook snoods, will be best.

Baits can be varied between what fish expect to find. Small ragworms previously dug from the mud when the tide ebbs, are suitable for most of the species. Small strips of mackerel or herring also make good offerings. With some species artificial lures and spinning tactics will score. The pollack and bass will grab eagerly at a spun bait.

Perhaps the hardest part of this form of sea angling is landing the fish successfully. Because of the height of the fisherman above water a dropnet is often necessary. Landing your catch becomes a two-man operation, one handling the rod and the other lowering and raising the capturing net. Take your time in playing out the fish as well as guiding it toward the net. Never attempt to net a fish that is still fighting.

Above left: Because of the inevitable rubbish that accumulates around a pier or in a harbour you will lose leads in the tangles. Lead is expensive, so scout around for cheap sinkers, spark-plugs, large nuts and bolts or even kidney-shaped stones will all get your bait down to where the fish are feeding!

84

Left: The best and safest way to land your fish from the pier. A dropnet has to be lowered by a companion fisherman. When you are sure that the fish is played out, steer it toward the already lowered net, which should be just below the water surface. As soon as the fish is safely within the net, the net is raised taking the weight of the fish off your rod and line.

Above: A useful and cheap rod for the pier. Made in solid glass fibre, 7 ft in length with stout rings, a rod like this will give years of pleasure. Make sure that both rod and reel are strong enough to land the fish — or better still, use a dropnet.

POUTING

Trisopterus luscus
Left: A small fish, of the cod family, that is found almost everywhere — over reefs, wrecks, outside harbour walls and at the rocky outcrops, that sprout from the shore. Fished for with light tackle, and small hookbaits, the fish can provide sport. If taken home and cooked soon after capture, the pouting provides a tasty meal. *Baits:* worms, small fish strips and shellfish presented close to the seabed.

Left: The baitdigger hard at work as the tide ebbs to reveal a patchwork of worm-casts.

Below: The sure signs of lugworm — a blow-hole and sand casts. The worm lives in a tunnel between them.

Right: Harbour walls make excellent fishing platforms but be careful — never hang over the edge or run about.

Angling in the estuaries

Where the saltwater meets freshwater running out from rivers and streams we find an odd mixture of angling. The estuaries, as they are called, provide fishermen with an area rich in fish and the feed that these fish seek. Silt washed down from the rivers is rich in minerals that encourage the growth of plants and at the same time provide excellent feeding ground for many tiny creatures like worms and cockles.

Bass, mullet and flounders search the estuary for food. They tolerate a high freshwater content and the last two named species can be found many miles up-river in totally freshwater. The narrow river mouth is easily fished as it can be covered with a bait from both sides over quite a large fishing area. The wide estuary does present difficulties. To fish it efficiently you would have to use a dinghy because the fish and feeding areas are more spread out. The ebbing tide cuts channels in the flat mud ground and it is in these channels that the fish are often found. A word of caution. Be very careful if you walk over tidal flats to reach these creeks and channels. There will be a number of parts made up of extremely soft mud into which you could sink. Also, the tide ebbs *and flows* quite quickly over the flats, hiding the channels from view, so make sure of the state of the tide before venturing out over the flats.

A light casting rod or carp-type float rod will handle both mullet and flounders. Of course, bass would give tremendous sport on either gear. Mullet can be fished for by trotting a small white ragworm on float tackle down the current. Use a technique similar to that of the freshwater angler when trotting on a river. Flounders can be taken on either float tackle or on a legered bait. They are fond of peeler crabs and marine worms. I like fishing a worm on a rolling leger. Casting across the creeks so that the current flow rolls the bait across the channel, where it covers a lot of ground searching out where the flounders are lying on the bottom.

I prefer to fish the in-coming tide on the basis that the tide is bringing fish in toward me and I have constantly to retreat back toward the safe ground. Mullet come in on a tide and may stay up in the creeks throughout the whole tidal phase. Look for them where the river opens out into large bays or creeks that join the main stream. They feed on minute plankton animals, grazing like sheep over the mudflats. Mullet are easily frightened, bankside noise or unnecessary splashing in the shallows will soon drive them away into quiet backwaters.

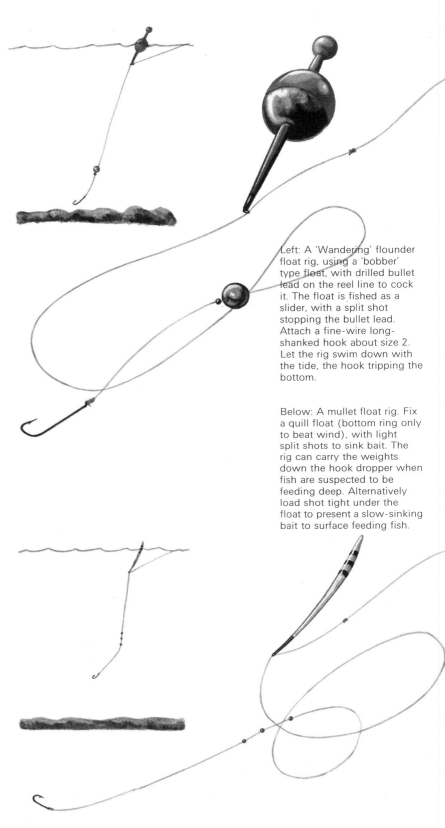

Left: A 'Wandering' flounder float rig, using a 'bobber' type float, with drilled bullet lead on the reel line to cock it. The float is fished as a slider, with a split shot stopping the bullet lead. Attach a fine-wire long-shanked hook about size 2. Let the rig swim down with the tide, the hook tripping the bottom.

Below: A mullet float rig. Fix a quill float (bottom ring only to beat wind), with light split shots to sink bait. The rig can carry the weights down the hook dropper when fish are suspected to be feeding deep. Alternatively load shot tight under the float to present a slow-sinking bait to surface feeding fish.

FLOUNDER

Platichthyes flesus
Right: A fish that is frequently found in the muddy estuaries, creeks and high up into river mouths in water that is almost completely fresh. Slimmer than the plaice, the flounder has a line of bony tubercles or bony scales along the base of both dorsal and anal fins, together with a similar line of bony plates behind the head. Some flounders will have bright orange spots similar to the plaice. *Baits:* most marine creatures, but worms and soft crabs are best.

MULLET (THICK-LIPPED)

Chelon labrosus
Left: Has a narrow throat gap, when the head is viewed from the underside, whereas the thin-lipped species has a wide throat gap. All mullets have two dorsal fins, the first of which has four sharp spines joined by strong skin webs. Mullet are shy fish and must be approached cautiously. *Baits:* small pieces of fish, marine worms and bread paste, preferably mashed up with an addition of pilchard oil.

Keep your tackle simple and do not carry too much gear with you. Estuary and creek fishing can involve a lot of hard walking so you do not want to be heavily laden. One item of gear that can be used to advantage is a pair of binoculars. The estuaries are a haven for a multitude of seabirds and waders. Even shelduck visit the flats and in winter there will be several species of geese that travel to our shores from the Arctic wastes. Come to know and recognize the birds that inhabit the mudflats.

On days when the fishing may not be too successful – when for various reasons the mullet and flounders refuse to take the bait – watching the bird life around you is adequate compensation and can add a great deal of pleasure to an angling day.

A mullet lagoon, in the South of Ireland.

Other species, big and small

There are several hundred species of sea fishes that will, at some time or other, enter the coastal waters of the western European shores. Many of these fish are of little commercial importance. Although not especially fished for as food for humans, a number of the fish species can give good or interesting sport to the angler as well as providing a tasty meal for the family.

A lot of the fish that pay us annual visits cannot be taken on a rod and line. The mighty basking shark, a fish of several tons weight, is a plankton feeder living by continuously sifting the smallest of creatures from the saltwater as the great shark swims in the tidal drift. Tiny gobies and blennies are so small that they are unable to accept a bait, presented on a hook, unless it is of the smallest size. More often than not these fish are taken in a shrimp net that is pushed into the weed growing in most tidal pools. Great fun can be had foraging, with a collecting net, in rockpools and saltwater lagoons. Catch the little fish, examine them carefully and return them to the habitat to continue their lives.

There are a few fish that will not appear in the catches of anglers or deep-sea trawlers. Species like the pipefish, weavers and immature specimens of the flat-fishes are most often caught by the beam netters that seek prawns and shrimps with fine-meshed nets. Among the mass of life that is pulled aboard the shrimp boats, after an hour's beam trawling, will be a superb collection of immature fish of all types, many rarely seen by fishers from the shore!

Fish come in families with each species varying just a little. Size, colour, shape of body and fins and known habitat are all keys to the identification of each different kind of fish. It is a good idea to buy a simple fish identifying guide, one that will slip into the pocket of your fishing jacket. When you catch a fish that is not instantly recognizable, examine it carefully, preferably whilst it is still wet. Pay particular attention to the position and number of fins, then look for peculiar colouration such as various spots, streaks or bands of lighter skin tone. Examine the teeth but make sure that the creature is quietened before attempting to open the mouth! If your specimen has spines handle it carefully for, although only two of our species are in anyway poisonous, a fish's spines can inflict a nasty wound that often takes a long time to heal.

As you know, most freshwater fish are kept, during the fishing session, in a keepnet. They

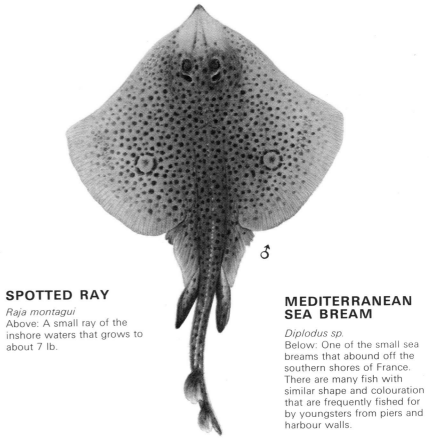

SPOTTED RAY

Raja montagui
Above: A small ray of the inshore waters that grows to about 7 lb.

MEDITERRANEAN SEA BREAM

Diplodus sp.
Below: One of the small sea breams that abound off the southern shores of France. There are many fish with similar shape and colouration that are frequently fished for by youngsters from piers and harbour walls.

are admired, weighed and possibly photographed by their captor before being returned to the water. We don't keep sea fish in a net. They can be placed in rock pools for a time but so often they die. This is because the temperature of the pool is much higher than that of the seawater, so it is probably a kindness to replace them in the sea as soon as you can.

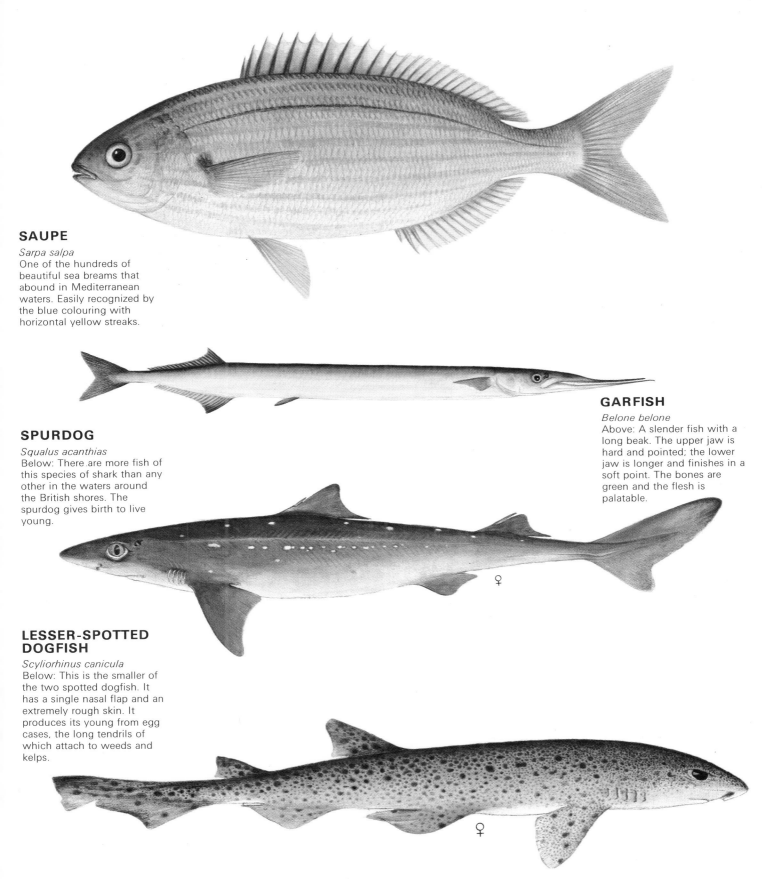

SAUPE

Sarpa salpa
One of the hundreds of beautiful sea breams that abound in Mediterranean waters. Easily recognized by the blue colouring with horizontal yellow streaks.

GARFISH

Belone belone
Above: A slender fish with a long beak. The upper jaw is hard and pointed; the lower jaw is longer and finishes in a soft point. The bones are green and the flesh is palatable.

SPURDOG

Squalus acanthias
Below: There are more fish of this species of shark than any other in the waters around the British shores. The spurdog gives birth to live young.

LESSER-SPOTTED DOGFISH

Scyliorhinus canicula
Below: This is the smaller of the two spotted dogfish. It has a single nasal flap and an extremely rough skin. It produces its young from egg cases, the long tendrils of which attach to weeds and kelps.

Colourful visitors

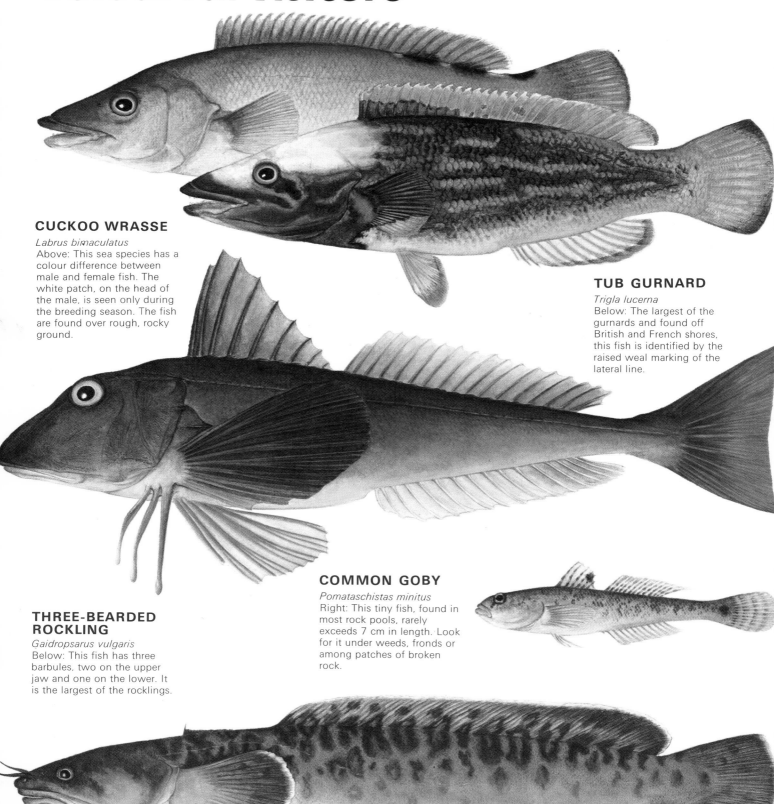

CUCKOO WRASSE

Labrus bimaculatus
Above: This sea species has a colour difference between male and female fish. The white patch, on the head of the male, is seen only during the breeding season. The fish are found over rough, rocky ground.

TUB GURNARD

Trigla lucerna
Below: The largest of the gurnards and found off British and French shores, this fish is identified by the raised weal marking of the lateral line.

THREE-BEARDED ROCKLING

Gaidropsarus vulgaris
Below: This fish has three barbules, two on the upper jaw and one on the lower. It is the largest of the rocklings.

COMMON GOBY

Pomataschistas minitus
Right: This tiny fish, found in most rock pools, rarely exceeds 7 cm in length. Look for it under weeds, fronds or among patches of broken rock.

GREATER WEAVER

Trachinus draco
Above: The spines on the first dorsal fin of this fish eject poisonous venom, and mean it should be handled with great care. The lesser species is equally dangerous.

PLAICE

Pleuronectes platessa
Right: This flatfish has bright orange spots on the coloured side. Its skin is smooth but it has a few bony lumps on its head, behind the eyes.

COALFISH

Pollachius virens
Left: Similar in appearance to the pollack, this member of the cod family has a white lateral line that is almost straight.

SHORT-SPINED SEA SCORPION

Myoxocephalus scorpios
Below: Often called the 'Father Lasher', this little fish is common around British shores. It is able to inflate the area around the throat to make a sound.

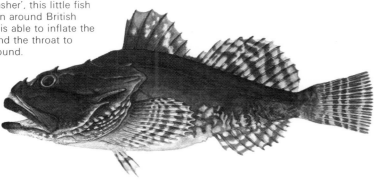

As the ocean currents move, in never-ending cycles, towards our coasts they bring fish and other forms of drifting life. There are both fish and minute plankton travelling in the warm current streams. Many of these forms of life are not very good swimmers. The ocean sunfish, for example, sways its body from side to side using the simple fin arrangement to maintain direction and keep itself in an upright position. There appears to be little planning as to where this fish goes! In late spring and into the summer the North Atlantic Drift will bring sunfish toward Britain because the fish is eating the creatures that are also drifting along northward. Some fish come up from warmer seas to spawn. They make annual migrations from Mediterranean waters to our offshore reefs to breed. They include sea breams, both red and black, together with lesser known members of that huge family of fishes.

The two eels, conger and freshwater, that live in the sea and rivers of our lands travel many miles on the ocean currents before arriving in Britain. Both species begin life in the Sargasso Sea, where they hatch from the eggs before becoming tiny leaf-like creatures. The eels spend up to three years drifting north toward us. Along the way they undergo a daily change, called metamorphosis, gradually becoming slim replicas of their parents.

It is all too easy to over-fish a particular species. The herring was a staple food in Britain and western European countries from the Middle Ages up to the Second World War. Then fishermen of all nations improved their gear and boats to the extent that the herring has all but disappeared from the North Sea. Even the mighty common skate came under pressure, this time from anglers. Far too many were hooked, landed and killed. But anglers recognized their mistakes, and in places like the Shetland Islands, skate are now returned to the water to grow larger and provide better sport for future sea anglers.

There is always a danger of polluting the environment. With the increasing number of oil tankers and North Sea oil rigs there will have to be a constant watch kept upon accidental spillage of the crude oil. The sea birds are at risk, even when they alight onto the water in mid-ocean. When wind-blown oil reaches our shores it can smother bait beds, fill the rock pools with muck and ruin the habitat for many years. If you see oil on the beach or rocks, inform the local police.

INDEX

Entries in italics indicate an illustration

A

Angling clubs 26
Anti-kink devices *56*
Artery forceps *56*, 58

B

Baits 14, 16, 18, 19, 22, 34,
50–51, 84
barley *19*
bread 16, *19*, 34, 41, 45, *51*
cereal 51
cheese *19*
coasters 55
floating *53*
gozzer 51
grasshoppers 22
mackerel *65*
maggots 9, 16, 22, 34, 41,
45, 50, 55
meat 20
sausage *19*
seed 20
shellfish *62*, *69*, *77*
slow sinking *48*
sweetcorn 55
tares *19*
weightlers *24*
worms 16, 18, *19*, 22, 25,
34, 40, 45, 50, *51*, 55, 70,
74
Bass 6, 69, *72*, 73, 74, 77,
86
Barbell 6, 7, 8, 12, *13*, 20
Barbules 12
Bleak 6, 7, *12*, 20, 21
Booms *67*
Bream 6, 7, 9, 12, 28, *29*,
38, 44, 48
Bronze 34, *35*
French Sea *88*
Mediterranean Sea 88
Silver 34
British Waterways Board 27
Burbot 7, 35, *37*

C

Canals 6, 26, *27*, 28, 29
Carbon dioxide 8
Carp 6, 8, *12*, 28, 30, 36,
38, 52–54, *53*
Crucian 54
Leather 35, *36*
Mirror *36*
Casting 16, 40, 46, *68*
Fly *49*
Overhead 25
Chub 6, 7, *10*, 18, *22*, 24, 30
Coalfish *91*
Cod *68*, 70, 78

D

Dab *70*, 72
Dace 6, 7, *11*, 18, 24, 49
Dapping 22, *23*, 24
Dogfish *74*
Lesser Spotted *89*
Dough bobbins *39*, 46

E

Eggs 10
Estuaries 6, 7, 63, 86, 87
Eels 10, 30, 76, *91*
Conger *78*

F

Fertilization 10
Finding the depth *17*
Fins 10
Fish, anatomy of *11*
Fish, skeleton of *11*
Float fishing 24, 38, 44–45,
48–49, 52, 53, 55
Floating crust 52
Floats *14*, 16, 18, *22*, 28, *29*,
39, 40, *49*, *55*, 58, *76*, 86
leger 48
lift 34
sea *76*
self-cocking 48
Flounder 6, 73, 74, *75*, 86,
87
spoon *74*
Food chain 8
Fly fishing 18, *49*

G
Gaffs *57*
Gags *56*, 58
Game fish
    See Salmon and Trout
Garfish *89*
Gill slit 8
Goby, Common *90*
GRP 14
Greater Weaver *91*
Groundbait 12, 16, 20, 24, 25,
    40, 42, *44*, 46, 48, *50*, 54
Gudgeon 7, *12*, 20, 28

H
Harbour fishing 84–85
Handlines *64*
Hatcheries 36
Hooks 14, 18, 21, 28, 34, 40,
    44, *47*, *53*, *54*, 55, 58, 65,
    66, *67*, 70, 75
    parts of *46*
Hybrids 6, 28, *29*

I
Ide *7*
Indicators, top bite 39
    quiver tip 16
Industrial Revolution 26
Insects 9, 33, 48
    See also Baits

K
Kinking 56
Knots
    blood loop *66*
    caster leader *66*
    double-blood loop *66*
    hook droppers *66*
    spade and whipping *18*
    tucked half blood *18*, 23

L
Lake fishing 30
Landing nets 23, 46, 57
Leads *15*, 19, 25, *69*
Legering 16, 24, 38, 42, *43*, *45*,
    46–47, 53, 59
Lift method 40, *41*
Lines 14, 18, 23, 28, 40, 74

Livebaiting 58, 59
Loach 12
    Stone 6, *13*
    Weather 7, *13*
Longtrotting 16, *17*, 18
Lures *21*, *56*, *77*, *79*, 80,
    82, *83*

M
Mackerel, 78, *79*, 91
    See also Baits
Maggots, *See* Baits
Miller's Thumb 6
Minnow 7, *12*
Monkfish 74
Mullet 6, 7
    Grey 7
    Thick-lipped *87*

N
Nase 7, *10*
Night fishing *45*

O
Orfe *35*
Overshotting *40*, *48*, 49
Oxygen 6, 8, 30, 32

P
Perch 6, 7, 8, *12*, 21, 28, 30,
    32, 36, 38, 54, 56, 57
Photosynthesis 8
Pike 6, 8, *12*, 21, 28, 30, 36,
    38, 52, 57, *58*, *59*
Plaice *91*
Plankton 12
Plants 8, 30, 32
    See also Weeds
Plumbing 40
Pole fishing *16*
Pollack 78, *79*
Pollution 91
Pouting *85*
Priest 82

R
Raking 40, *41*
Reels 14, *15*, 24
    centre pin 14, *15*, 16, 64
    fixed spool 14, *15*, 16, 38, 64,
    74, 84
    multiplier 64, *74*, 84

Rigs, barbel 20
   basic shore-fishing *67*
   bream and carp fishing *46*
   Continental-style *28*
   crucian carp *55*
   dart fleet *28*
   float leger *38, 42*, 74
   mullet float *86*
   nylon link leger *29*
   nylon paternoster *74*
   paternoster livebait *58*
   perch paternoster *54, 74*
   pier paternoster *84*
   pole fishing *28*
   rolling leger *19*
   sink and draw *59*
   sliding float *76*
   terminal 48
   wandering flounder float *86*
   wire running *74*
Rings *15*
Roach 6, 7, *10*, 16, *22*, 24, 28, 37, 38, 54
Roach pole *15*, 16
Rock fishing *62*
Rockling 78
   Three Bearded *90*
Rods 14, 18, 24, 66, *85*
   bass *75*
   beach *65*
   float 14, *15*
   fly fishing *49*
   leger 14, *15, 38*
   spinning 14, *15, 78*
   still water *38*
   telescopic *15*
Rod rests 46
Rudd 6, 9, 29, *34*, 38, 48
Ruffe 6

S Salmon 6, 8, 10, 12, *13*, 30, 38, 52
Sargasso Sea 10, 30
Saupe *89*

Shorefishing 60–82
Short Spined Sea Scorpion *91*
Skate *91*
Small stream fishing 22
Smelt 7
Spinners *21*
Spools 14, *38, 68*
Spotted Ray *88*
Spurdog *89*
Stillwater fishing 30–39
Strettpegging 16
Swimfeeders *24, 25*
Swimming the stream *17*, 28

T Tackle *83*
Tench 6, 8, 28, 30, 34, *35*, 38, 40, 42, 44
Thornback Ray *72, 73*
Tope 72, 74
Trotting *22*
Trout 6, 8, 22, 26, 30, 36
   Brown *13*, 30
   Rainbow 30, *36*
   Sea *13*
Tub Gurnard *90*

W Water layers 32–33
Water Beetle 33
Water Scorpion 33
Weeds 6, 8, *33*, 34
   See also Plants
Whiting 68
Wind speeds 60
Worms *See* Baits
Wrasse, Ballan 76, *78*, 79, *81*
   Cuckoo *90*

Z Zander 21, 30
Zope 6, *13*